Report of the Federal Trade Commission on the news-print paper industry : June 13, 1917.

Report of the Federal Trade Commission on the news-print paper industry : June 13, 1917.
Multiple Contributors, See Notes
collection ID CTRG96-B1114
Reproduction from Harvard Law School Library
Washington : G.P.O., 1917.
162 p. ; 25 cm

The Making of Modern Law collection of legal archives constitutes a genuine revolution in historical legal research because it opens up a wealth of rare and previously inaccessible sources in legal, constitutional, administrative, political, cultural, intellectual, and social history. This unique collection consists of three extensive archives that provide insight into more than 300 years of American and British history. These collections include:

Legal Treatises, 1800-1926: over 20,000 legal treatises provide a comprehensive collection in legal history, business and economics, politics and government.

Trials, 1600-1926: nearly 10,000 titles reveal the drama of famous, infamous, and obscure courtroom cases in America and the British Empire across three centuries.

Primary Sources, 1620-1926: includes reports, statutes and regulations in American history, including early state codes, municipal ordinances, constitutional conventions and compilations, and law dictionaries.

These archives provide a unique research tool for tracking the development of our modern legal system and how it has affected our culture, government, business – nearly every aspect of our everyday life. For the first time, these high-quality digital scans of original works are available via print-on-demand, making them readily accessible to libraries, students, independent scholars, and readers of all ages.

old books. new life.

The BiblioLife Network

This project was made possible in part by the BiblioLife Network (BLN), a project aimed at addressing some of the huge challenges facing book preservationists around the world. The BLN includes libraries, library networks, archives, subject matter experts, online communities and library service providers. We believe every book ever published should be available as a high-quality print reproduction; printed on-demand anywhere in the world. This insures the ongoing accessibility of the content and helps generate sustainable revenue for the libraries and organizations that work to preserve these important materials.

The following book is in the "public domain" and represents an authentic reproduction of the text as printed by the original publisher. While we have attempted to accurately maintain the integrity of the original work, there are sometimes problems with the original work or the micro-film from which the books were digitized. This can result in minor errors in reproduction. Possible imperfections include missing and blurred pages, poor pictures, markings and other reproduction issues beyond our control. Because this work is culturally important, we have made it available as part of our commitment to protecting, preserving, and promoting the world's literature.

GUIDE TO FOLD-OUTS MAPS and OVERSIZED IMAGES

The book you are reading was digitized from microfilm captured over the past thirty to forty years. Years after the creation of the original microfilm, the book was converted to digital files and made available in an online database.

In an online database, page images do not need to conform to the size restrictions found in a printed book. When converting these images back into a printed bound book, the page sizes are standardized in ways that maintain the detail of the original. For large images, such as fold-out maps, the original page image is split into two or more pages

Guidelines used to determine how to split the page image follows:

• Some images are split vertically; large images require vertical and horizontal splits.
• For horizontal splits, the content is split left to right.
• For vertical splits, the content is split from top to bottom.
• For both vertical and horizontal splits, the image is processed from top left to bottom right.

REPORT

OF

THE FEDERAL TRADE COMMISSION

ON THE

NEWS-PRINT PAPER INDUSTRY

JUNE 13, 1917

WASHINGTON
GOVERNMENT PRINTING OFFICE
1917

SENATE RESOLUTION NO. 87.

[Reported by Mr. Smith, of Arizona.]

In the Senate of the United States,
June 19 (calendar day June 20), 1917.

Resolved, That the report on the news-print paper industry, submitted by the Federal Trade Commission on June 13, 1917, in response to Senate resolution 177, Sixty-fourth Congress, be printed as a Senate document, and that 5,000 additional copies be printed for the use of the Senate Document Room.

Attest:

James M. Baker,
Secretary.

2

CONTENTS.

CHAPTER III.—PRICES OF NEWS-PRINT PAPER.

CHAPTER IV.—JOBBERS' COMMISSIONS AND MARGINS OF GROSS PROFIT.

CHAPTER V.—COSTS AND PROFITS OF MANUFACTURE.

Chapter VI.—SUPPLY AND DEMAND FACTORS.

Chapter VII.—EVIDENCE OF VIOLATIONS OF THE ANTITRUST LAWS.

Chapter VIII.—SUMMARY OF PRINCIPAL FACTS WITH CONCLUSIONS AND RECOMMENDATIONS.

LIST OF TABLES.

6

LIST OF EXHIBITS.

———

8

ACKNOWLEDGMENT.

The Commission desires to mention as especially contributing to the preparation of this report Messrs. E. O. Merchant, Le Claire Hoover, and William T. Chantland. Messrs. F. L. Hawes, W. R. Bendz, W. W. Bays, J. K. Arnold, H. L. Anderson, W. P. Sterns, J. H. Bradford, and A. R. Peterson also rendered valuable assistance.

9

LETTER OF SUBMITTAL.

FEDERAL TRADE COMMISSION,
Washington, June 13, 1917.

To the PRESIDENT OF THE SENATE:

The Federal Trade Commission has been engaged upon an investigation of the news-print paper industry pursuant to Senate resolution 177, Sixty-fourth Congress (Senator Owen), adopted April 24, 1916, and there is submitted herewith its complete report. A preliminary report was submitted on March 3, 1917, which contained a summary of the Commission's activities and findings in connection with the investigation and which recited the efforts of the Commission through processes of accommodation and arbitration to restore competitive conditions in the industry and to insure a fair price to consumers of news-print paper while the processes of restoration were going forward. This preliminary report, with some revisions, has been incorporated in the complete report and will be found in Chapter VIII, which contains the conclusions and recommendations of the Commission.

INCREASED PAPER COST.

The consumption of news print paper in the United States in 1916 amounted to about 1,775,000 net tons, valued at more than $70,000,000. At the prices now prevailing this tonnage will cost news-print consumers in 1917 more than $105,000,000, an increase of $35,000,000, or 50 per cent. Most of this increase will fall upon newspaper publishers. If the average increase in cost of manufacture in 1917 over 1916 is estimated at $10 per ton, which is liberal, one-half of the $35,000,000 increase in paper cost represents additional profits to the manufacturers.

FAILURE OF ARBITRATION AGREEMENT.

The efforts of the Commission to restore competitive conditions in the news-print industry expeditiously and to arbitrate and effectively project a fair price for news-print paper have failed. Since the arbitration agreement referred to in the preliminary report was entered into with some of the manufacturers of news-print paper and since the award of the Commission fixing a fair price for news-print

11

paper was announced a Federal grand jury for the southern district of New York, partially upon evidence furnished by the Commission, has found indictments against four of the signatories to such arbitration agreement for violations of the Sherman antitrust law and the said indictments are now pending for trial. From the time the arbitration agreement was signed and the award made, and prior thereto, the Commission has bent every effort to bring about some practical relief to this situation. The plan failed for several reasons, the principal reason being that the arrangement was voluntary and the Commission had no power or warrant under the law to make it effective. Several of the manufacturers signatory to the agreement, subsequent to the finding of the indictment in this matter notified the Commission that they would not proceed under such arbitration agreement, The result has been that news-print paper has been billed and sold at the same exorbitant prices that obtained in many instances theretofore.

PRESENT SITUATION SERIOUS

The news-print paper situation is very serious, not only to the consumers of paper but to the public generally and to the Government of the United States, which is itself a large consumer of paper. The Commission has reason to believe that this situation will be still more aggravated and serious in the ensuing months. In normal times competitive conditions would have been gradually restored through the processes of law, but it would have required some time to translate the effect into the prices of paper. The demand for news-print paper is constantly increasing and gives promise of still greater increase with the continuance of the war. The supply of news-print paper available to meet this demand is dependent upon mills already in existence. This supply will probably not exceed the quantity produced last year and may be less owing to disturbances that may result from the war. Under normal conditions it takes from twelve months to two years to bring a new paper mill into operation. Under present conditions it would take much longer. It seems probable, therefore, that with the demand for news-print paper increasing and the supply remaining constant or possibly diminishing there will be a repetition of the panic market of last year and the exaction of prices that are entirely out of measure with the cost of production. The consequences to thousands of smaller newspapers and to many of the larger ones, and through them to the reading public, will be most serious.

WAR EMERGENCY MEASURE RECOMMENDED.

By reason of this condition, and because of the vital interest to the public of an efficient dissemination of news in this crisis, the

Commission recommends as a war emergency measure that Congress by appropriate legislation provide:

(1) That all mills producing and all agencies distributing print paper and mechanical and chemical pulp in the United States be operated on Government account; that these products be pooled in the hands of a Government agency and equitably distributed at a price based upon cost of production and distribution plus a fair profit per ton.

(2) That pursuant thereto some Federal agency be empowered and directed to assume the supervision and control thereof during the pendency of the war.

(3) That, by reason of the fact that approximately 75 per cent of the production of news-print paper in Canada comes into the United States, proper action be taken to secure the cooperation of the Canadian Government in the creation of a similar governmental agency for the same function, which shall be clothed with power and authority to act jointly with the governmental agency of the United States for the protection of the consumers and manufacturers of print paper and the public of the United States and Canada.

(4) That, in case the Canadian Government shall not join in such a cooperative enterprise, then importation of paper and mechanical and chemical pulp into the United States shall be made only on Government account to or through the Federal agency charged with such supervision and distribution.

In this connection the Commission desires to point out that such a plan contemplates the operation of mills under their present management and the use of the present distributing agencies, but that such use and operation shall be for the public good, directed by a disinterested public agency to secure equitable distribution and a price that is based upon a fair cost of production and a fair profit per ton to be determined without regard to the panic market created by unusual and abnormal conditions. This plan has the virtue of being analogous to those plans which have been tried and successfully operated in Great Britain. It will also insure the maximum production and greatest facility in transportation and distribution and will adapt itself readily to a return to normal competitive conditions upon the conclusion of the war.

Respectfully submitted.

WILLIAM J. HARRIS, *Chairman.*
JOSEPH E. DAVIES.
WILLIAM B. COLVER.
JOHN FRANKLIN FORT.

CHAPTER I.

INTRODUCTION.

Section 1. Origin of investigation.

The investigation of the news-print paper industry was made by the Commission pursuant to the following resolution of the Senate of the United States:

> *Resolved*, That the Trade Commission is hereby requested to inquire into the increase of the price of print paper during the last year, and ascertain whether or not the newspapers of the United States are being subjected to unfair practices in the sale of print paper.[1]

During the first session of the Sixty-fourth Congress complaints from publishers resulted in the introduction of various resolutions in both Houses of Congress calling for an investigation of the rise in prices of news-print paper. These complaints came mainly from the smaller publishers not protected by contracts, who were the first to feel the increase in prices.

Trade papers early in 1916 pointed out a probable increase in consumption on account of the demand for advertising space, and warned publishers of a possible scarcity. On April 5, at the instance of the News-Print Manufacturers Association, a conference was held in New York between representatives of the manufacturers and publishers to discuss the paper situation. The purpose of the manufacturers in seeking this conference was afterwards set forth by the secretary of the association in an interview appearing in the Editor and Publisher, October 7, 1916, as follows:

> We were approaching a crisis, and, unless something was done to curtail the demand, to conserve the supply, we could see that there would be a shortage that would seriously affect newspapers, not only with regard to the quantity they might desire, but as to the price, for it must be perfectly apparent to any reasonable man that where there is a shortage of material—a demand in excess of the supply, with first one and then the other bidding at a higher rate to get what the other fellow wants and must have—that increased prices naturally result.

Nothing was accomplished by the conference.

---

[1] S. Res. 177, 64th Cong., 1st sess., adopted Apr. 24, 1916.

Section 2. Petition of news-print manufacturers.

On May 6, 1916, shortly following the adoption of the Senate resolution above referred to, the News-Print Manufacturers Association made formal appearance before the Commission by its secretary and attorneys, who presented a petition signed by the executive committee of the association,[1] and asked that—

> as soon as it can be done an investigation be had by your body into this question in accordance with the Senate resolution above set forth; and these petitioners respectfully state that they will consider it a privilege to furnish this Commission any information within its power.

Under date of May 9, 1916, the secretary of the association reiterated the desire of both Canadian and United States members to cooperate with the Commission in the following statement:

> It is our earnest desire that this investigation of the news-print paper manufacturing industry shall be so thorough and complete that it may not be necessary to make further investigations of this sort for some time to come, and to that end we tender you all the facilities of our organization, and hope that our assistance may facilitate the investigation both in point of time and expense.

The cooperation of the members of the association and also of several domestic companies not belonging to the association, all of which voluntarily opened their books to the Commission's accountants and agents and furnished all the information desired, greatly expedited the progress of the investigation, and also made it possible to study the industry in Canada as well as in the United States.

Section 3. Cooperation of publishers' associations.

The American Newspaper Publishers Association, National Editorial Association, Association of Pennsylvania Dailies, and others have cooperated with the Commission in this investigation. Their representatives attended the various hearings called by the Commission to discuss the news-print paper situation, and their officers were active in urging members to supply information called for by schedules of questions which the Commission sent to newspaper publishers.

Very commendable work has also been done by the officers of these associations in urging members to disallow the return of unsold papers by newsdealers, to eliminate waste, and to curtail consumption. Early in March, 1916, the manager of the American Newspaper Publishers Association called the attention of the members to the reduced stocks of news-print paper and higher current prices, and suggested serious consideration of economy in the use of paper. A month later a bulletin was issued declaring that reserve stocks were "at or

---

[1] For full text see Exhibit 1.

about the danger line," and urging that "every economy should be made in the use of news print until the mills have had an opportunity to replenish their reserve." In subsequent bulletins publishers were continually urged to eliminate waste and curtail consumption. This association has also inaugurated campaigns for saving waste paper and wrapping paper which have had important results.

The propaganda spread by publishers' associations, trade papers, etc., has apparently accomplished much good. Reports from all parts of the country indicate that since about the middle of 1916 many publishers have been working individually and in cooperation to eliminate wastes and to reduce their consumption to the minimum required by the news and advertising matter.

In a bulletin issued by the American Newspaper Publishers Association, dated October 21, 1916, it was announced that 540 papers had reported that they no longer allowed papers to be returned. Moreover, 90 had increased their selling price and 21 had advanced advertising rates.

In response to its letter of October 14, 1916, encouraging and urging economy of news-print paper, especially in Sunday editions, the Federal Trade Commission received within two weeks over 100 responses from publishers announcing their adherence to the proposed policy and stating in nearly all instances that they had already instituted some economies.[1]

In this connection attention should be called to the success of the New York Globe in meeting increased paper costs by the introduction of various economies and the adoption of more efficient methods based on a knowledge of costs. The publisher of this newspaper issued a pamphlet in February, 1917, giving the results of his experience and study of methods to meet the abnormal news-print situation.[2]

Section 4. Scope of investigation.

Owing to the importance of reporting its conclusions as quickly as possible, the Commission limited its inquiry in this investigation to the subjects especially pertinent to the determination of the causes of the present increase in price. In Chapter II, however, are presented some data of a general nature regarding the news-print industry which will be of value to the reader in reaching a better understanding of the price question.

PRICE INQUIRY.—The first inquiry of the Commission was to determine to what extent prices of news-print paper had risen in different localities. For this purpose agents of the Commission collected a

---

[1] For extracts from these letters, see Exhibit 2.
[2] Newspaper Efficiency, by Jason Rogers.

mass of price data from the sales records of the manufacturers, selling agencies, and jobbers. Prices were also furnished by a large number of newspaper publishers throughout the country in response to a schedule of questions sent out by the Commission. The results obtained by this branch of the investigation are presented in Chapter III, which shows the contract and open-market prices to publishers in different localities in 1916 as compared with previous years.

The price statistics obtained from jobbers enabled the Commission to ascertain their rates of commission and margins of gross profit in 1916 as compared with prior years. These data are presented in Chapter IV.

COST INQUIRY.—One of the important questions involved in this investigation was whether the increase in prices was justified by the increase in the cost of manufacture. To determine this question the Commission sent its agents to the offices of most of the manufacturers in the United States and Canada and obtained the cost figures from January 1, 1913, to June 30, 1916, directly from the books of the companies, together with full information regarding the method of handling costs. The Canadian manufacturers belonging to the News-Print Manufacturers Association through courtesy furnished the Commission with the same information as was furnished by the United States companies. Costs have also been secured for a part of the second six months of 1916.

Considerable difficulty was experienced in this phase of the investigation owing to the lack of uniformity in cost systems of different companies. In a few cases the records of the companies were so incomplete that it was impossible to ascertain their costs.

In addition to obtaining cost figures for the three and one-half years ending June 30, 1916, the Commission secured information regarding the profits of the manufacturers and their investments in plants and woodlands. This was considered important in order to ascertain whether prices prior to the recent rise had been too low, as was claimed, and had yielded too small a return upon the investment in the business. It was very difficult, on account of the character of the records and the limited time for conducting the investigation, to determine accurately the real investment of the news-print companies. The book investments, as a rule, threw little light on this question because of inflations growing out of amalgamations, reorganizations, etc.

The data regarding costs and profits are presented in Chapter V.

SUPPLY AND DEMAND FACTORS.—In arriving at its conclusions regarding the causes of the increase in prices it was necessary for the Commission to ascertain what changes had taken place in the relation of supply to demand during the year 1916. For this investigation of economic causes production, shipment, and inventory figures were obtained from the manufacturers for the years 1913 to 1916, inclusive. Inventory figures were also obtained from jobbers. The publishers of daily papers were asked to furnish figures showing the receipts of paper and inventories for different dates, and most of them furnished such figures as they could. Circulation figures were obtained from the sworn returns of publishers to the Post Office Department and statistics of advertising were obtained for the principal newspapers in several of the largest cities.

The information collected by the Commission relative to the supply and demand factors is presented in Chapter VI.

ACTIVITIES OF MANUFACTURERS AND JOBBERS.—For the investigation of alleged unfair or illegal activities of manufacturers and jobbers the Commission's agents not only examined the contracts of all of the principal manufacturers, selling agencies, and jobbers, but also the correspondence files of the News-Print Manufacturers Association and some of the more important members. Publishers also furnished a considerable amount of valuable information relative to this matter.

The findings of the Commission regarding this phase of the investigation are presented in Chapter VII.

CONCLUSIONS AND RECOMMENDATIONS.—The conclusions of the Commission were contained in its preliminary report to the Senate dated March 3, 1917, and are repeated in Chapter VIII of this report. The Commission's recommendations for the protection of publishers during the continuance of the present abnormal conditions resulting from the war are contained in the letter of submittal above and also in Chapter VIII.

Section 5. Efforts for immediate relief of publishers.

An important fact brought out by the news-print paper investigation was that most of the output of low-cost mills was sold under annual contracts to the large publishers of the country, while many of the 2,000 small dailies and some 14,000 weeklies depended on the open market or on high-cost mills for their supplies of news print. In the latter part of 1916 these smaller papers in many cases had extreme difficulty in obtaining a supply of paper except at prices which, if maintained, would have driven them out of business.

The public hearing of the Commission on December 12, 1916, made this situation so clear that at the opening of the afternoon session, the manufacturers through their attorney requested suggestions from the Commission as to some method of distributing their available product that would take care of the small publishers. The willingness of the associations of small publishers to forward some such scheme of distribution was at once made evident. At the same time their representative said "We do not believe we can get this help or this assistance unless it be through the cooperation of the Federal Trade Commission as a mediary in this particular emergency."

In accordance with its established policy in cases where its assistance is requested in cooperative efforts of business men to improve competitive conditions, the Commission in pursuance of the above suggestion arranged for conferences of committees representing publishers, manufacturers and jobbers. As a result of these conferences the Commission at the close of the year instituted a thorough canvass, which revealed very completely the immediate needs of newspaper publishers without contracts. The manufacturers and large publishers, however, were unable to come to any agreement through which a supply of paper could be secured for distribution to small publishers under the supervision of the Commission. As the Commission had no legal powers through which the necessary paper could be obtained it was compelled to abandon this effort to furnish immediate relief.

On January 26, 1917, a conference between manufacturers and publishers was held in Chicago at which the suggestion was made that the Federal Trade Commission should arbitrate the question of what was a fair and reasonable price for the sale of news-print paper. Adopting this suggestion, several manufacturers in February, requested the Commission to determine what was a fair price for standard news for the six-month period beginning March 1, 1917, and agreed to abide by its decision. After conferences with publishers and jobbers the Commission decided to undertake this task, and on March 4, 1917, announced the prices which it had determined in a report to the Senate of the United States.[1] Subsequent to this announcement, various complications arose which caused the plan to fail. The details of these later developments are given in Chapter VIII. (See p. 140.)

---

[1] Senate Doc. No. 3, 65th Cong., special session.

CHAPTER II.

GENERAL DESCRIPTION OF THE NEWS-PRINT PAPER INDUSTRY.

Section 1. Introduction.

There are some 2,500 daily and Sunday and about 14,000 weekly and semiweekly newspapers in the United States. The daily papers, according to Census data for 1914, had a circulation of about 30,000,-000 copies, the Sunday papers about 17,000,000, and the weeklies and semiweeklies about 24,000,000. These newspapers range from the largest metropolitan daily, with an average circulation for the six months ending October 1, 1916, of more than 800,000 copies per day, to the smallest country weekly, with a circulation of a few hundred copies each week. These dailies and weeklies together furnish the cheapest and most serviceable means of disseminating information, general and local, to the 100,000,000 people in this country. Practically every town of any size in the country has at least one publication devoted especially to local affairs. For this reason the great reading public has a special interest in whatever affects the welfare of these publications.

DAILY NEWSPAPERS.—The 2,500 daily newspapers, nearly 600 of which have Sunday editions, have nearly 60 per cent of the total circulation of all newspapers and consume the great bulk of the news-print paper produced and imported.[1] There are 119 daily news-papers in 32 of the 50 cities having 100,000 population or over, which have an average daily circulation in excess of 50,000, according to sworn statements to the Post Office Department for the six-month period ending October 1, 1916. These 119 dailies have a total circulation of 15,649,634 copies. The following tabulation groups them according to circulation:

Group.	Number of publications.	Combined circulation.
400,000 and over..	6	2,914,626
300,000–400,000..	5	1,887,568
200,000–300,000..	9	1,979,432
100,000–200,000..	35	4,431,269
50,000–100,000...	64	4,436,739
Total...	119	15,649,634

[1] More than 1,000 daily newspapers also have weekly or semiweekly editions.

These 119 daily newspapers represent about 50 per cent of the total circulation of dailies. There are 430 other newspapers in the United States having an average daily circulation of 10,000 or more whose combined circulation is estimated at 7,500,000 and about 1,900 dailies having less than 10,000 circulation with an estimated total of 9,000,000.

One hundred of the daily newspapers in the United States, or 4 per cent, are published in the two cities of New York and Chicago and have a combined circulation of nearly 6,500,000, or about 20 per cent of the total.

Practically all of the daily papers use roll news, most of which is bought on contract.

WEEKLY NEWSPAPERS.—The 14,000 weekly and semiweekly newspapers use sheet news largely and purchase it in the open market. On account of the large expense necessary to the gathering of news and miscellaneous matter for the make-up and printing of such papers, about 6,000 of the smaller weekly newspapers make use of what is known as "ready print service." They buy their paper already printed on one side or on two or more pages, and print the rest of the paper themselves, using local news items. In addition to the ready print service many of them use what is known as "plate service" which is news matter furnished in the form of metal type plates cast in column lengths which may be cut up and arranged at the local office if desired.

There are several concerns which make a business of furnishing ready print or plate services to publishers. The most important of these are the Western Newspaper Union, Omaha, Nebr.; the American Press Association, New York City; and the American Type Founders Co., Jersey City, N. J. Other important ones are the Publishers Press Association, Toledo, Ohio; United Weekly Press Association, of Grand Rapids, Mich.; and Publishers Cooperative Co., Chicago. The Western Newspaper Union has 30 branch offices located in as many cities of the United States, extending from Boston to Denver and Minneapolis to Houston. It supplies more than 90 per cent of the papers using ready print and in addition furnishes large quantities of plate service to other publishers. At each of its offices it does more or less printing of weekly newspapers, trade journals, magazines, etc., for other publishers. At the Chicago office alone about 120 such publications are printed. In addition to being the largest consumer of sheet news print in the United States, it is also an important factor as a paper jobber, carrying stocks of printing paper at nine of its branch offices and doing some jobbing business in sheet news at each of its other branches. The jobbing business at Omaha is conducted under the trade name of Western Paper Co.

Section 2. Development of the news-print industry.

The manufacture of paper from wood pulp dates back to the sixties, when the first machine for grinding wood was installed in this country. Prior to this time the paper used for printing newspapers was made of rags, straw, and other vegetable fibers. Poplar was the first wood used for making pulp, and then spruce. The latter has been found the most satisfactory of all of the woods for making news print and is at present the most extensively used.

With the use of wood pulp for making news print there came a rapid development in the industry. The estimated daily capacity of domestic news-print mills increased from about 400 tons in 1880 to about 4,700 tons in 1916. According to the United States Census reports, the quantity manufactured in domestic mills since 1899 and the value of the product has been as follows:

Year.	Tons produced.	Value of product.	Year.	Tons produced.	Value of product.
1899	569,212	$20,091,874	1909	1,175,554	$46,855,560
1904	912,822	35,906,460	1914	[1] 1,313,284	52,942,774

[1] This figure includes about 30,000 tons of paper not classed by manufacturers as news print. The Commission's production figure for 1914 was 1,282,934 tons.

The production of news-print paper in the calendar year 1916, December being estimated, was 1,355,196 tons.

RANK OF INDUSTRY.—The United States Census reports for 1914 rank the paper and wood-pulp industry of the country as twentieth in total value of products. News-print paper constituted about one-fourth of the total paper tonnage shown, and somewhat less than one-sixth of the total value. Other important grades of paper manufactured are book, writing, wrapping, tissue, kraft, bag, etc. The total production of the 45 United States companies making news-print paper in 1916 was found by the Commission to be 1,355,196 tons, valued at more than $50,000,000. Of this paper about 75,000 tons were exported and most of the remainder was used by newspapers. In addition, they also used nearly 468,000 tons of Canadian paper, which was about 75 per cent of the total production of that country. The commercial uses of news-print paper are largely for catalogues, telephone directories, railway guides, school tablets, handbills, wrapping paper, etc.

PERIOD PRIOR TO 1910.—In the decade prior to 1900 the rapid building of paper mills led to overproduction and a decline in prices. In 1898 the International Paper Co. was organized. It absorbed most of the mills east of the Mississippi River, with the control of from two-thirds to three-quarters of the domestic output. For two or three years after the organization of this combination prices were firmer, but new mills were being built, and by 1901 prices again began a downward movement, which reached the lowest point in 1906. The net earnings of the International Paper Co. fell from $3,961,657 in the year ending June 30, 1901, to $1,623,616 in 1906–7. A representative of the company testified that the average gross receipts per ton on its sales had fallen from $42.52 in 1901 to $39.90 in 1906? The following year the average receipts per ton advanced to $41.

In the latter part of 1907 and early in 1908 a great effort was made to advance prices further. It was to some extent successful, and the increase in the cost to some newspapers was very considerable. This resulted in the appointment of a committee of the House of Representatives, which, after a very full investigation beginning in the spring of 1908, made its final report to Congress in February, 1909. This report emphasized the scarcity of spruce in the United States and the need for its conservation. It recommended that ground wood should be admitted free from territory in which there was no restriction on exports and that the duty on news print be reduced to one-tenth cent per pound. On this point the report reads as follows:

> It can not be expected that Canada or its Provinces will remove the present discriminations as to the exportation of pulp wood to the United States or cease from adding additional discriminations unless we also lessen the tariff on the cheap paper, which is made mainly from spruce wood.

The committee held that the duty of $2 per ton recommended by it would offset the high cost of production in the United States.

PERIOD SUBSEQUENT TO 1910.—Since 1910, although prices remained above the 1906 level, the news-print industry in the United States has barely held its own, only one large mill having been built. On the other hand, several mills have been changing machines over from news print to other grades, especially since 1913, the aggregate loss to news-print production since 1910 probably amounting to 500 tons a day. As a result there was a decline in the output in 1914 and 1915, and prices also showed a downward trend. (See pp. 61 to 68.)

In 1916 some revival occurred in the development of the domestic industry. Prices rose and production increased more than 100,000 tons over the preceding year. Before the close of 1916 the International Paper Co. completed the installation of two new machines with a combined capacity of about 62 tons per 24-hour day, and three additional machines with a combined daily capacity of 140 tons began operations in other mills during the first half of 1917.

In marked contrast with the stationary condition of the news-print industry in the United States during the last five years has been the phenomenal development of the industry in Canada. Between 1910 and 1916 six new mills operating 10 machines were built, with an estimated daily capacity of more than 500 tons. This increased output of news print was largely exported to the United States. One new machine with a daily capacity of 50 tons began operation in November, 1916, and several new developments are under way which will begin operations in 1917 and 1918.

According to a report of the American Newspaper Publishers Association of March 24, 1917, the new tonnage expected in the United States and Canada during 1917 and 1918 is as follows:

New tonnage, 1917 (revised Mar. 22):	Tons per day.
Hawley Pulp & Paper Co., now running	50
Great Northern Paper Co., now running	50
Spanish River Pulp & Paper Mills—	
Now running	35
November	50
St. Maurice Paper Co.—	
Now running	50
April	50
Pacific Mills (Ltd.)—	
July	60
October	60
Price Bros. & Co.—	
November	65
May	50
Northwest Paper Co., April	50
Brompton Pulp & Paper Co., December	50
Ontario Paper Co.—	
Now running	50
November	50
Abitibi Power & Paper Co., December	175
Mill organizing, December	50
	945

Tonnage for 1918 (revised Mar. 22):	
Laurentide Co. (Ltd.), Grand Mere, Province of Quebec, November	200
Price Bros. & Co., Kenogami, Province of Quebec, November	175
Lake Winnipeg Paper Co., November	200
Mill organizing, November	200
	775

Future tonnage (uncertain as to time and quantity):	
International Paper Co., Three Rivers, Province of Quebec	200
Pic River and Nipigon Power	150
Kenora, Ontario (E. W. Backus)	200
	550

The St. Maurice Paper Co. at Three Rivers, Quebec, is a subsidiary of the Union Bag & Paper Co. The Pacific Mills (Ltd.), at Ocean Falls, British Columbia, is a subsidiary of the Crown Willamette Paper Co.

There is some doubt whether the mills reported as beginning operations in November and December, 1917, will be completed by that time. They represent a daily capacity of 440 tons.

Section 3. Process of production.

The basic material in the manufacture of paper is cellulose, which is obtained in the form of plant fibers. In the case of news-print paper the fibrous material is obtained from certain kinds of wood. Spruce is most generally utilized, though hemlock, balsam fir, and other kinds are used in some cases. The wood is cut usually in winter and transported to the mill, when practicable, by floating the logs down a stream. Shipment to the mill by rail and water also is employed extensively.[1]

The first step in the process after the logs have arrived at the mill is that of removing the bark if this has not already been done. This is accomplished by one of two types of machines. The first type is called the tumbler, which consists of a large cylindrical drum. Into this drum the logs, in 2-foot lengths, together with a suitable quantity of water, are introduced. The drum is then caused to revolve, and the friction of the logs against the side of the drum and against one another removes the bark. The second type is called a barker, or rosser, and consists of a heavy iron disk, provided usually with three knives fixed to its surface and projecting about half an inch from it. The disk is rotated rapidly and when the logs are pressed against its surface the bark is shaved off by the knives.

The second is the more thorough method but is less economical, because of the loss of the wood which is cut away. Sometimes the logs are barked before they are shipped to the mill in order to save freight.

After being barked the pieces of wood are converted either into "mechanical" pulp or into "chemical" pulp. The former is not suitable alone for paper making because it contains only about 55 per cent of cellulose and the fibers are too short and stiff to felt or interlace together properly; hence it is mixed with a certain quantity of chemical pulp which is pure cellulose with fibers of greater length.

MECHANICAL PULP.—Mechanical pulp or ground wood is produced by applying the pieces of wood by hydraulic pressure to the face of a large grindstone, usually about 54 inches in diameter and 27 inches

---

[1] For a description of the process of the production of paper, see the Pulp and Paper Magazine, Jan. 4, 1917, pp. 11–28.

thick. This grindstone rotates at a high rate of speed within a casing, which is provided with pockets into which the pieces of wood are introduced and pressed against the stone. If sufficient water is introduced into the pit of the grinder the temperature can be kept about at normal, but the usual practice in this country is to limit the quantity of water admitted, so that the friction brings about high temperatures. Experiments are reported to have been successfully carried out with the lengthwise grinding of logs in order to obtain a longer fiber in the ground wood. An important improvement in ground wood equipment is the magazine grinder now in use in one mill in the United States and one in Canada. This grinder feeds the wood in automatically from above and not only economizes in floor space but also in labor costs. The wood grinders are operated almost exclusively by water power, the grindstones frequently being attached directly to the turbine shaft. In other cases they are propelled by electricity.

The ground wood comes from the grinders in the form of slush, which is then screened in order to remove the coarser particles. In the older mills this screening is done in small troughs with fine screen plates in the bottom. Rotary screening is now coming into general use. The slush is run into a revolving cylinder with screen plates in its surface. The centrifugal force throws the finer particles of slush through these screens. One great advantage of this system is that the installation requires much less room than the older one.

After the slush has been screened it is ready to be used for paper making. Where the ground wood mill is a part of the paper mill or not too far distant from the paper mill the ground wood slush is piped in without converting into pulp. Where it is necessary to ship the ground wood by rail it is compressed until from 30 to 50 per cent of the water is squeezed out.

CHEMICAL PULP.—Spruce wood, in addition to cellulose, contains a considerable amount of nonfibrous material, which is dissolved and separated from the cellulose by cooking the wood under pressure with a solution of bisulphite of lime. This is known as the sulphite process. The wood is first chipped up into small pieces by a machine which consists of a massive iron or steel disk about 84 inches in diameter with two or three steel knives projecting from the surface of this disk and radiating from the center. This disk is caused to revolve rapidly, and the logs are applied to the surface of the disk, usually at an angle of 45°. The knives then chip off flakes of wood from the end of the log at that angle.

There are two methods of preparing bisulphite of lime for use in the sulphite process, designated, respectively, the "tower" system and the "tank" system. In the tower system, which is in most general use, sulphur is burned in specially constructed ovens with a limited amount of air so as to form sulphur dioxide gas. This is run out through pipes, which enter into a tank of water to cool the gas and then into tall towers, usually of wood, with a lining of lead. These towers may be considerably over 100 feet in height and from 5 to 10 or more feet in diameter. The towers are filled with blocks of limestone, and a continuous stream of water is introduced from the top of the tower. As the gas passes upward through the limestone it enters into combination with the water and lime, so that the liquid flowing out at the bottom of the tower is a solution of bisulphite of lime.

In the tank system, otherwise called the "milk-of-lime" system, water and lime are mixed in a large vat, and the sulphur-dioxide gas is forced into the mixture to form bisulphite of lime. The process varies in detail, of course, from plant to plant. An amount of sulphur approximating from 300 to 350 pounds is required in the production of a ton of air-dry pulp.

The chemical process of making sulphite is conducted in large boilers, commonly called "digesters." These may be of varying type, but the one in almost universal use is a tall cylindrical vessel, sometimes being of sufficient size to produce from 11 to $16\frac{1}{2}$ net tons of pulp. The digesters are constructed of boiler plate and are lined with acid-resisting brick or tile set in acid-proof mortar. This, of course, is to prevent the acid developed in the process from corroding the metal of which the digester is constructed, but has also the further advantage of effecting a considerable saving in steam, because of the fact that this lining acts as a heat insulator. The digesters taper to a cone at the top and bottom ends.

The process of cooking varies considerably in different plants. In general, after the chips of wood and the bisulphite of lime have been introduced, the manhole is closed, and steam is gradually forced in at the bottom. This is continued until the steam pressure reaches about 80 pounds and the temperature about 365°.[1] The process of cooking is continued about eight hours. At the end of the cooking process the outlet at the bottom of the digester is opened, and the steam pressure quickly forces the material out into a large bin with a screen bottom, through which the liquid drains off. At this point the pulp usually is washed for about three hours by means of water delivered at the top of the bin. The ligneous and resinous portions of the wood, being in solution, to great extent are washed away. Spruce-wood pulp obtained in this manner contains about 88 per cent of cellulose, while untreated spruce wood contains only about 55 per cent.

---

[1] Dept. of Com., Bur. of For. & Dom. Com., Special Agents Series, No. 110, p. 47.

Following this the chemical pulp is screened to remove coarse fibers, knots, slivers, and the like, in much the same manner as the mechanical pulp.

PAPER MAKING.—The paper-making process proper begins in the "beaters," where the various component substances of the finished product are mixed.

The beaters are large receptacles of various types, the important common characteristic of which is a cylindrical roll fitted with steel or bronze blades, which revolves over a stationary concave bedplate equipped with similar blades. The pulp is caused to circulate in the vat so that all of it will pass under this roll about an equal number of times. At the beginning of the operation the roll is raised slightly above the bedplate and then gradually lowered as the operation is continued, until the fibers have been sufficiently torn apart, and the various ingredients have been thoroughly mixed.

In the case of news-print paper the proportion of mechanical to chemical pulp varies according to the quality of the paper desired, type of machines, etc. On the average about 80 per cent of mechanical pulp is mixed with about 20 per cent of chemical pulp. Various other ingredients are also introduced, such as talc or china clay which is used as a filler to render the paper more opaque, and to give it a smoother surface, and liquid rosin, which is used to "size" the paper so that the printing ink will not be absorbed and thus cause the impressions to become blurred. Red and blue aniline dyes are added, when obtainable, to make the paper white. Alum is also added to precipitate the rosin and the coloring matter upon the fibers.

Owing to the greater cost of sulphite ordinarily only a sufficient quantity is used to give the news print such tensile strength that it will run through the paper machines and the printing presses without breaking.

In some plants the beating process is shortened somewhat by the use of the so-called Jordan refining engine. This machine consists of a hollow cone equipped on its interior surface with blades and another smaller cone with blades on its exterior surface. The smaller cone revolves within the larger one, and the pulp is reduced to the desired consistency by the action of the blades against each other.

After the beating process has been completed the pulp, very much diluted with water, is run into a so-called stuff chest, in which it is kept in constant motion to prevent the pulp from settling to the bottom. From this chest the pulp or slush passes through a strainer and into a long narrow box placed at the head of, and across the full width of, the paper machine. Thence it overflows onto a wire-screen belt consisting of fine copper wires, woven with 60 or 70 meshes to the inch. The length of this screen is often 75 feet and the width 150 or more inches. This belt moves forward on a series of 3-inch rolls, and also has a lateral shaking motion. The pulp settles down upon this screen in the form of a wet sheet, much of the water draining through the mesh of the screen. Toward the farther end of the screen it passes over several vacuum boxes, which cause still more moisture to be sucked out through the screen. The speed at which the screen is run is as high in some cases as 680 feet per minute.

When the slush is run onto the wire screen difficulty is caused by reason of the fact that the speed of the slush is less than that of the screen. This has a tendency to cause ripples in the sheet to be formed. This difficulty has been obviated for the most part by the use of a new principle of operation known as the Eibel process, patented in 1907, in accordance with which the screen is inclined, so that the sheet is carried in a downhill direction. The action of the force of gravity thus causes the sheet to maintain the same speed as the screen, and the screen merely supports the sheet.

At the end of the screen the sheet passes between two rolls called the couch rolls, the upper one of which is covered with a felt jacket. From the screen belt the sheet runs onto a woolen belt. Thence it passes between a series of so-called press rolls, the purpose of which is to squeeze out further quantities of water. Finally, the sheet is run over several large hollow cast-iron cylinders 3 or 4 feet in diameter, heated internally by steam. These rolls dry the paper thoroughly. The sheet then passes through the calendar rolls, which polish the surface, and is wound upon a roll. The rolls of paper later are removed and rewound upon cores, the paper being trimmed and cut to the proper width at the same time. They are then removed to the finishing room, where they are wound with heavy wrapping paper to protect them in shipment.[1]

Section 4. Domestic and Canadian companies.

There were on January 1, 1916, about 45 companies in the United States engaged in the manufacture of news-print paper, which together operated 63 mills, and 15 companies in Canada, which together operated 17 mills. Ten of the United States companies did not have sulphite plants and four did not have either sulphite or ground-wood plants. All of the Canadian companies but one had ground-wood mills, but four did not have sulphite plants.

---

[1] For a description of the parts of a paper machine, see Paper, Apr. 26, 1916, pp. 13-16.

The International Paper Co., which is the largest manufacturer in the United States, has 9 mills which are operated almost entirely on news print and 2 or 3 mixed mills, making other grades as well as news. These mills are located in Maine, New Hampshire, Vermont, Massachusetts, and New York.

The Great Northern Paper Co., which is the next largest manufacturer in the United States, has 2 news-print mills located at Millinocket and East Millinocket, Me., and 1 mixed mill, which makes some news, located at Madison, Me.

The Minnesota & Ontario Power Co. operates a large mill at International Falls, Minn., and controls the Fort Frances Pulp & Paper Co. (Ltd.), in western Ontario, Canada. The Crown Willamette Paper Co. operates 2 mills located at West Linn, Oreg., and Camas, Wash., and also controls the Pacific Mills Co. (Ltd.), which has a new mill about ready to begin operations at Ocean Falls, British Columbia.

These four large companies in 1916 produced about 55 per cent of the total domestic output.

The largest Canadian manufacturer is the Spanish River Pulp & Paper Mills (Ltd.), which controls the Lake Superior Paper Co. (Ltd.). The combined companies have 3 mills making news print, located at Sault Ste. Marie, Sturgeon Falls, and Espanola, Ontario, Canada. The next largest Canadian manufacturers are the Laurentide Co. (Ltd.), at Grand Mère, Quebec; Powell River Co. (Ltd.), at Powell River, British Columbia; Price Bros. & Co. (Ltd.), at Kenogami and Jonquière, Quebec; and the Abitibi Power & Paper Co. (Ltd.), at Iroquois Falls, Ontario, which did not begin operation on news until the middle of 1915.

PRODUCTION AND SHIPMENTS.—The tons of news-print paper produced and shipped by the principal companies in the United States and Canada and the total production and shipments of all mills in each country are shown in Table 1 below for the calendar years 1913, 1914, 1915, and 1916. The figures for the companies shown in detail and for some others were obtained directly from their books. Some of the figures included in the item "all others" were obtained by correspondence with the manufacturers. The companies are arranged in order of tons produced in 1916. Every company known to have produced any news print during the 4-year period has been included in the total figures.

TABLE 1.—PRODUCTION AND SHIPMENTS OF NEWS-PRINT PAPER BY PRINCIPAL
UNITED STATES AND CANADIAN COMPANIES, 1913-1916.

Companies.	1913		1914	
	Production.	Shipments.	Production.	Shipments.
United States:	Tons.	Tons.	Tons.	Tons.
International Paper Co.	402,763	423,106	379,810	379,542
Great Northern Paper Co.	150,082	147,242	169,082	172,317
Crown Willamette Paper Co.	80,343	78,190	75,777	80,000
Minnesota & Ontario Power Co.	65,181	65,435	64,124	63,028
Remington Paper & Power Co.	44,954	43,674	45,914	46,583
De Grasse Paper Co.	35,146	35,196	40,872	40,872
Berlin Mills Co.	62,334	62,880	51,583	52,013
St. Croix Paper Co.	37,012	37,626	40,311	40,733
Pejepscot Paper Co.	35,000	35,000	23,406	24,293
Consolidated Water Power & Paper Co.	29,439	29,577	30,428	29,884
Finch, Pruyn & Co. (Inc.).	32,250	32,367	30,677	31,356
St. Regis Paper Co.	36,009	37,720	41,512	42,383
Tidewater Paper Mills Co.	26,848	27,338	27,492	27,060
Gould Paper Co.	19,217	18,497	23,668	22,313
All others (31 companies).	241,987	240,015	238,278	235,750
Total United States.	1,304,595	1,313,263	1,282,934	1,287,986
Canada:				
Spanish River Pulp & Paper Mills (Ltd.).	[1]109,000	[1]105,000	118,884	118,332
Powell River Co. (Ltd.).	43,959	39,140	44,767	45,552
Laurentide Co. (Ltd.).	62,269	61,919	64,260	64,439
Price Bros. & Co. (Ltd.).	26,369	24,602	42,808	42,754
Belgo-Canadian Pulp & Paper Co. (Ltd.).	36,380	36,392	36,465	36,358
Fort Frances Pulp & Paper Co. (Ltd.)[2]	....	....	16,067	15,033
J. R. Booth.	35,355	34,313	37,015	36,916
Donnacona Paper Co. (Ltd.).	....	....	7,480	9,317
All others (6 companies).	37,115	37,115	47,236	47,236
Total Canada.	350,447	338,481	414,982	415,937
Total[3] United States and Canada.	1,655,042	1,651,744	1,697,916	1,702,923

[1] Estimated.
[2] Subsidiary of Minnesota & Ontario Power Co.
[3] These totals may include a very small tonnage of paper other than news print.

TABLE 1.—PRODUCTION AND SHIPMENTS OF NEWS-PRINT PAPER BY PRINCIPAL UNITED STATES AND CANADIAN COMPANIES, 1913-1916—Continued.

Companies.	1915		1916[1]	
	Production.	Shipments.	Production.	Shipments.
United States:	Tons.	Tons.	Tons.	Tons.
International Paper Co..............................	340,236	344,549	373,263	383,448
Great Northern Paper Co...........................	181,880	188,720	197,533	193,677
Crown Willamette Paper Co........................	76,958	80,218	14,089	103,977
Minnesota & Ontario Power Co....................	59,096	60,583	87,042	87,441
Remington Paper & Power Co......................	33,110	32,053	49,426	49,550
De Grasse Paper Co................................	46,598	47,831	43,909	43,909
Berlin Mills Co...................................	44,869	45,675	40,882	42,017
St. Croix Paper Co................................	40,638	41,117	39,193	39,263
Pejepscot Paper Co................................	37,277	38,015	38,709	38,649
Consolidated Water Power & Paper Co.............	35,481	35,638	36,916	37,155
Finch, Pruyn & Co. (Inc.)........................	32,731	33,950	32,383	32,705
St. Regis Paper Co................................	22,249	26,791	31,116	31,493
Tidewater Paper Mills Co..........................	27,151	27,223	28,798	28,729
Gould Paper Co....................................	26,088	26,110	25,767	25,253
All others (31 companies)........................	234,830	239,741	236,273	238,923
Total United States...............................	1,239,122	1,268,200	1,355,196	1,374,221
Canada:				
Spanish River Pulp & Paper Mills (Ltd.)..........	115,289	115,434	130,436	132,931
Powell River Co. (Ltd.)...........................	50,307	51,100	64,113	65,307
Laurentide Co. (Ltd.).............................	65,648	65,573	63,037	62,806
Abitibi Power & Paper Co. (Ltd.)[3]..............	17,971	16,866	62,071	62,053
Price Bros. & Co. (Ltd.)..........................	47,279	45,318	53,523	55,893
Belgo-Canadian Pulp & Paper Co. (Ltd.)..........	38,204	38,155	50,725	51,166
Fort Frances Pulp & Paper Co. (Ltd.)[3].........	31,696	32,487	39,430	39,497
J. R. Booth......................................	35,363	35,300	38,679	38,658
Donnacona Paper Co. (Ltd.)........................	14,470	14,685	18,242	17,733
All others (6 companies).........................	72,414	75,567	87,720	88,179
Total Canada.....................................	488,621	490,485	607,976	614,226
Total [4] United States and Canada...............	1,727,743	1,758,685	1,963,172	1,988,447

[1] The production and shipments for the month of December, 1916, were estimated by the companies.
[2] Began operations in 1915.
[3] Subsidiary of Minnesota & Ontario Power Co.
[4] These totals may include a very small tonnage of paper other than news print.

The table shows that the 14 United States companies having an output of more than 25,000 tons each in 1916 produced in the aggregate more than 82 per cent of the total domestic production, while the 31 smaller companies included in the item "all others" produced less than 18 per cent. Likewise in 1916 the 9 Canadian companies shown in the table produced more than 85 per cent of the Canadian production, while the remaining 6 companies produced less than 15 per cent.

The four largest companies in the United States in 1916 produced the following percentages of the total domestic production and of the total production on the North American Continent:

88569°—17——3

Company.	Tons produced.	Percentage of United States output.	Percentage of output of North American Continent.
International Paper Co...	373,203	27.0	19.0
Great Northern Paper Co..	197,533	14.0	10.1
Crown Willamette Paper Co...,...................	94,039	6.9	4.8
Minnesota & Ontario Power Co....................................	87,042	6.4	¹ 0.4
Total..	751,927	55.5	40.3

¹ Including 39,430 tons of the Fort Frances Pulp & Paper Co. (Ltd.) of Canada, a subsidiary of the Minnesota & Ontario Power Co.

The Spanish River Pulp & Paper Mills (Ltd.), which was the largest Canadian manufacturer in 1916, produced 130,436 tons of news-print paper, or 21.5 per cent of the total Canadian output and 6.6 per cent of the total output of the North American Continent.

Domestic production decreased about 65,000 tons during the years 1913 to 1915. The production for the whole year 1916, December being estimated, exceeded that of 1913 by about 50,000 tons and that of 1915 by 116,000 tons. This was accomplished in spite of an actual decrease in the number of mills in operation.

Canadian production increased about 138,000 tons during the years 1913 to 1915, and the 1916 production, December being estimated, was about 120,000 tons greater than for the preceding year. This great increase in production was accomplished chiefly by building new mills and adding new machines to old mills. More than 75 per cent of the Canadian output finds a market in the United States.

The total production for United States and Canada in 1916, December being estimated, was nearly 1,964,000 tons, or an increase of more than 235,000 tons over 1915. This increase is equivalent to nearly 760 tons a day, allowing 310 working days a year.

Shipments showed movements similar to those of production. In general they were slightly larger than the tonnage produced, owing in part to some duplication caused by companies buying from one another, which could not be eliminated, and in 1915 and 1916 to a decrease in stocks on hand.

EQUIPMENT.—Table 2 below shows the equipment of the ground-wood, sulphite, and paper mills of the 16 largest United States news-print manufacturers and the 11 largest Canadian manufacturers on January 1, 1916. These figures were compiled from Post's Paper Mill Directory, Lockwood's Directory of the Paper and Stationery Trades, and from information obtained directly from the companies. The figures for the maximum 24-hour capacity of grinders, digesters, and paper machines are estimates. The ratings for the paper machines are those used by the News Print Manufacturers' Association in its statistical reports. The ground-wood and sulphite equipment of most of the companies shown is in excess of the news-print requirements, some of these materials being sold or used in making other grades of paper. The Fourdrinier paper machines, on the other hand, are those running wholly or partly upon news print.

TABLE 2.—EQUIPMENT OF 16 UNITED STATES MANUFACTURERS AND 11 CANADIAN MANUFACTURERS OF NEWS-PRINT PAPER IN 1916.

Companies.	Ground wood.			Sulphite.			News print.		
	Mills.	Grinders.	24-hour capacity.	Mills.	Digesters.	24-hour capacity.	Mills.	Paper machines.	24-hour capacity.
United States:			*Tons.*			*Tons.*			*Tons.*
International Paper Co	23	273	1,276	8	44	470	12	50	1,500
Great Northern Paper Co	4	102	410	2	17	290	3	14	604
Crown Willamette Paper Co	5	81	366	4	16	205	2	8	250
Minnesota & Ontario Power Co.	1	24	168	1	4	120	1	2	220
De Grasse Paper Co	1	24	125	1	4	35	1	4	175
Berlin Mills Co	1	30	150	1	4	120	1	3	160
St. Croix Paper Co	1	22	175	1	2	60	1	3	131
Pejepscot Paper Co	2	26	140	1	4	35	2	4	132
Consolidated Water Power & Paper Co	2	24	60	....	....	....	2	4	120
Remington Paper & Power Co.	3	36	180	1	3	42	3	5	158
Finch, Pruyn & Co. (Inc.)	1	20	137	....	....	....	1	3	100
Tidewater Paper Mills Co	....	....	....	....	....	....	1	2	72
St. Regis Paper Co	3	23	200	2	6	90	1	4	145
Gould Paper Co	4	20	114	1	3	45	1	3	84
Northwest Paper Co	2	17	93	1	2	50	1	2	62
Wisconsin River Paper & Pulp Co	1	11	60	....	....	....	1	2	55
Total, 16 U. S. companies	54	743	3,654	24	109	1,472	34	113	3,994
Canada:									
Spanish River Pulp & Paper Mills (Ltd.)	3	60	390	2	4	135	3	10	444
Laurentide Co. (Ltd.)	1	37	250	1	4	110	1	6	200
Abitibi Power & Paper Co. (Ltd.)	1	20	250	1	2	60	1	4	225
Powell River Co. (Ltd.)	1	24	220	1	2	50	1	4	225
Price Bros. & Co. (Ltd.)	3	36	240	1	2	60	2	4	180
J. R. Booth	1	26	160	1	4	125	1	3	135
Belgo-Canadian Pulp & Paper Co. (Ltd.)	1	22	160	1	2	50	1	4	127
Fort Frances Pulp & Paper Co. (Ltd.)	1	15	100	....	....	....	1	2	150
Donnacona Paper Co. (Ltd.)	1	12	75	1	1	30	1	1	50
Brompton Pulp & Paper Co. (Ltd.)	2	41	240	....	....	....	1	1	55
Canada Paper Co. (Ltd.)	1	12	50	....	....	....	1	1	40
Total, 11 Canadian companies	16	305	2,135	9	21	620	14	40	1,831
Total, 16 United States and 11 Canadian Companies	70	1,048	5,789	33	130	2,092	48	153	5,825

The 16 largest domestic manufacturers, whose combined output represents more than 85 per cent of the total production of the United States, together operated 54 ground-wood mills equipped with 743 grinders, 24 sulphite plants equipped with 109 digesters, and 34 paper mills having 113 Fourdrinier machines running on news print. Some of these companies had other mills and other machines not running on news print. Three of these large companies did not have sulphite plants, and one did not have either a sulphite or ground-wood mill.

The 11 Canadian manufacturers operated 16 ground-wood mills equipped with 305 grinders, 9 sulphite plants equipped with 21 digesters, and 14 news-print mills equipped with 40 paper machines. Three of the companies did not have sulphite plants, but all were equipped with ground-wood mills.

The 24-hour capacity of mills shown in the table is considerably in excess of the actual production of news print, since this is a maximum figure and also since some of the machines are only run part of the time on this grade. For instance, in 1916 the International Paper Co. produced at the rate of 1,200 tons per day, allowing 310 working days in the year, although shown in the table as having a capacity of 1,500 tons.

The speed, in feet per minute, and the maximum width of sheet in inches, of the 113 paper machines operated on news print by 16 United States companies, is shown by the following tabulation:

SPEED PER MINUTE AND MAXIMUM WIDTH OF TRIM OF 113 PAPER MACHINES OF 16 UNITED STATES COMPANIES, 1916.

Speed per minute.	Number of machines.	Width of trim.	Number of machines.
300 to 399 feet	11	70 to 79 inches	14
400 to 424 feet	4	80 to 89 inches	9
425 to 449 feet	7	90 to 99 inches	10
450 to 474 feet	15	100 to 109 inches	13
475 to 499 feet	10	110 to 119 inches	15
500 to 524 feet	14	120 to 129 inches	10
525 to 549 feet	5	130 to 139 inches	6
550 to 574 feet	22	140 to 149 inches	27
575 to 599 feet	9	150 to 159 inches	3
600 to 649 feet	14	160 to 169 inches	5
650 to 699 feet	2	170 to 179 inches	1

Eleven of the machines of the 16 principal domestic companies had a speed of less than 400 feet per minute and 36 others had a speed less than 500 feet per minute. Fifty had a speed between 500 and 600 feet and 16 a speed above 600 feet. Thirty-three of the machines had a maximum trim of less than 100 inches, 71 machines had a maximum trim between 100 and 150 inches, and 9 machines had a trim above 150 inches.

The newer machines, as a rule, have a wider trim and higher speed than the older machines, so that the above figures are a good index of the character of the equipment of the principal manufacturers.

For comparative purposes the speed of machines and width of sheet are given in the tabulation below for the 40 Fourdrinier machines operated on news print by the 11 principal Canadian manufacturers:

SPEED PER MINUTE AND MAXIMUM WIDTH OF TRIM OF 40 PAPER MACHINES FOR 11 CANADIAN COMPANIES, 1916.

Speed per minute.	Number of machines.	Speed per minute.	Number of machines.
475 to 499 feet....................	1	575 to 599 feet....................	5
500 to 524 feet....................	3	600 to 624 feet....................	19
525 to 549 feet....................	0	625 to 649 feet....................	4
550 to 574 feet....................	1	650 to 699 feet....................	7

Width of trim.	Number of machines.	Width of trim.	Number of machines.
80 to 89 inches....................	1	140 to 149 inches....................	11
90 to 98 inches....................	1	150 to 159 inches....................	5
100 to 109 inches....................	4	160 to 169 inches....................	0
110 to 119 inches....................	7	170 to 179 inches....................	6
120 to 129 inches....................	0	180 to 189 inches....................	1
130 to 139 inches....................	2	190 to 199 inches....................	2

The tabulation shows that 30 of the 40 machines operated by Canadian companies have a speed above 600 feet per minute, and 25 of the 40 machines have a trim above 140 inches. These figures do not include the new machine of the Donnacona Paper Co., which began operations on November 1, 1916. This machine is said to have a speed of 600 to 625 feet per minute and a maximum width of sheet of 148 inches.

CONSUMPTION OF RAW MATERIALS.—Information obtained from 12 principal United States companies and 9 principal Canadian companies shows that in 1915 they used the following quantities of sulphite and ground wood in producing news-print paper:

Companies.	News print produced.	Ground wood used.		Sulphite used.		Percentage of sulphite to total pulp.
		Total.	Quantity per ton of paper.	Total.	Quantity per ton of paper.	
	Tons.	Tons.	Tons.	Tons.	Tons.	
12 United States companies..............	954,892	767,458	0.804	224,652	0.235	22.6
9 Canadian companies....................	416,207	328,302	.789	109,445	.263	25.0
Total, 21 companies combined.......	1,371,099	1,095,760	.799	334,097	.244	23.4

The 12 United States companies produced 77 per cent of the total domestic output of news-print paper in 1915 and the 9 Canadian companies more than 85 per cent of the total Canadian output. United States companies used on the average 0.804 of a ton of ground wood and 0.235 of a ton of sulphite in making a ton of paper. Canadian companies used 0.789 of a ton of ground wood and 0.263 of a ton of sulphite, and United States and Canadian companies combined used 0.799 of a ton of ground wood and 0.244 of a ton of sulphite in a ton of paper.

The average percentage of sulphite to total pulp used for United States and Canadian companies combined was 23.4 per cent. The average for domestic mills was 22.6 per cent and for Canadian mills 25 per cent. Applying the proportions of the two raw materials used by the principal companies to the total production of news-print paper in the United States and Canada, a fairly close estimate is obtained of the total quantity of ground wood and sulphite used by all companies in both countries in making news-print paper in 1915. This is shown by the following tabulation:

Companies.	News print produced.	Ground wood used.	Sulphite used.
	Tons.	Tons.	Tons.
All United States companies..	1,239,122	995,897	291,521
All Canadian companies..	488,621	385,375	128,487
Total United States and Canadian companies combined	1,727,743	1,381,272	420,008

The wide variation existing in the percentage of sulphite to total pulp used by different companies is shown by Table 3, which presents the data for 12 principal United States companies and 9 principal Canadian companies for 1915 and the first half of 1916.

TABLE 3.—PERCENTAGE OF SULPHITE TO TOTAL PULP FOR 12 PRINCIPAL UNITED STATES COMPANIES AND 9 PRINCIPAL CANADIAN COMPANIES, 1915-1916 (FIRST HALF).

United States companies.	1915	First half 1916.	Canadian companies.	1915	First half 1916.
1.................................	33.4	34.5	1.................................	27.2	28.3
2.................................	28.4	31.2	2.................................	24.9	27.4
3.................................	26.4	28.5	3.................................	25.9	....
4.................................	28.4	27.6	4.................................	25.8	25.2
5.................................	24.8	23.1	5.................................	25.3	24.7
6.................................	22.0	21.3	6.................................	23.9	24.0
7.................................	22.2	20.6	7.................................	23.7	23.7
8.................................	21.3	20.3	8.................................	23.9	23.4
9.................................	18.9	19.5	9.................................	21.3	23.3
10.................................	18.9	18.7	Average...................	25.0	25.0
11.................................	23.7	14.9	Average for 12 United States and 9 Canadian companies.	23.4	23.3
12.................................	13.3	12.8			
Average...................	22.6	22.4			

The table shows that the percentage of sulphite used by the 12 United States mills in the first half of 1916 ranged from 12.8 per cent to 34.5 per cent with an average of 22.4 per cent, and by the 9 Canadian mills from 23.3 per cent to 28.3 per cent with an average of 25 per cent. The percentage of sulphite necessary to make paper is affected by the method of treating ground wood, the character of the equipment, etc. The paper must have sufficient tensile strength to run through the paper machines without breaking, otherwise the daily output of the machines will be reduced. This fixes a minimum below which it is not economical to reduce the percentage of sulphite used.

The 12 United States mills taken together used slightly less sulphite in the first half of 1916 than they did in 1915, while the Canadian mills used the same proportion in each period. Information obtained from some of the United States companies for a part of the second half of 1916 indicates that there was a further decrease in the percentage of sulphite used during that period.

From data collected by the Commission an estimate has been made of the average quantity of rough wood used by news-print companies in making sulphite, ground wood, and news-print paper in 1915. Peeled wood and rossed wood have been converted to the rough-wood basis by using the best estimates available. Reports from the 12 United States companies and the 9 Canadian companies show the following results:

Companies.	Cords used in ton of ground wood.	Cords used in ton of sulphite.	Cords used in ton of news-print paper.
12 United States companies..	1.08	2.12	1.36
9 Canadian companies..	1.16	2.15	1.43
Total, 21 companies combined................................	1.10	2.13	1.40

If the percentages shown in the preceding tabulation for 21 companies are applied to the total production of ground wood, sulphite, and news-print paper for all companies in the United States and Canada, the total cords of rough wood used would be as follows:

Companies.	Cords of wood used in ground wood.	Cords of wood used in sulphite.	Cords of wood used in news-print paper.
All United States companies..	1,073,834	617,170	1,691,004
All Canadian companies..	447,497	276,135	723,632
Total United States and Canadian companies combined......	1,521,331	893,305	2,414,636

Considerable variation exists in the quantities of wood used by different companies in producing a ton of paper. For instance, reports from companies in the United States show that considerably over half of the paper included in the tabulation above was produced from about 1¼ cords of rough wood per ton, although one company which produced a little over 8 per cent of the paper used about 1¾ cords per ton. In this connection it is important to note that the use of a large quantity of wood does not necessarily mean a high wood cost per ton of paper, because, as a rule, the cheaper the wood the more freely it may be used. For example, the detailed figures for two of the large producers show that in 1915 one used 42 per cent more wood than the other, while the cost of its wood per ton of paper was only 15 per cent greater. In the first half of 1916 it used more than 42 per cent more wood, while the cost of its wood per ton of paper was only 6 per cent greater than that of the other producer. Both companies produced their paper at a very low cost.

It is to be noted also that if the present high prices of wood continue, processes of manufacture that economize wood will probably be adopted. The possible economy in wood through such processes is indicated by the following excerpt from the Paper Trade Journal of November 30, 1916, which relates to a recently invented but well-tested process:

> The quantity of final rejection is very small, 200 tons of finished paper showing a yield of sand, knots, bark, etc., of about 200 pounds, when using 140 cords of peeled spruce to produce the 200 tons of paper.

By this process apparently a ton of paper can be produced from 0.7 of a cord of peeled spruce (about 0.8 of a cord of rough wood) as compared with 1.40 cords shown above.

Section 5. News-Print Manufacturers Association.

The News-Print Manufacturers Association is a voluntary association organized April 1, 1915, and composed of nearly all the important news-print and hanging paper manufacturers on the North American Continent. Prior to 1915 these manufacturers constituted a division of the American Paper & Pulp Association.

The secretary of the association is George F. Steele, whose principal duty is to accumulate and disseminate to members information concerning materials, processes, machinery, improvements, etc., and statistical data covering stocks on hand, quantities produced, and quantities shipped.

The News-Print Manufacturers Association is managed by an executive committee of five members, who represent 51 per cent of the total output of all its members, which in 1916 represented about 82 per cent of the total production of news print in the United

States and Canada. The members of the executive committee and the 1916 output of news print represented by each are shown in the tabulation below:

Members of executive committee.	Name of company.	Position in company.	1916 production.
			Tons.
Philip T. Dodge........	International Paper Co..........................	President.....	373,263
George H. Mead.......	Spanish River Pulp & Paper Mills (Ltd.)...........	.....do........	
	The Lake Superior Paper Co. (Ltd.)..............	.....do........	130,436
	The George H. Mead Co., Dayton, Ohio............	.....do........	
	Sales agent for the above and also for the Abitibi Power & Paper Co. (Ltd.)........	....	62,071
J. M. A. Acer..........	Laurentide Co. (Ltd.).............................	Treasurer and sales manager.	63,037
E. W. Backus........	Minnesota & Ontario Power Co...................	President.....	57,042
	Fort Frances Pulp & Paper Co. (Ltd.).........	.....do........	39,430
G. H. P. Gould........	Gould Paper Co..................................	.....do........	25,767
	St. Regis Paper Co.[1]..........................	.....do........	31,116
	Donnacona Paper Co. (Ltd.).....................	.....do........	18,242
	Total represented by executive committee...	....	830,404

[1] This company was sold in December, 1916.

The total production of news-print paper on the North American Continent in 1916, as shown by Table 1, above, was 1,963,172 tons. Of this tonnage, 1,616,307 tons, or more than 82 per cent of the total, were produced by members of the association.

The principal companies outside of the association, and their production in 1916, were as follows:

Companies outside association.	Production in 1916.
Companies connected with newspapers:[1]	*Tons.*
Ontario Paper Co. (Ltd.), (Chicago Tribune)................................	
DeGrasse Paper Co. (New York World).................................	82,741
News Pulp & Paper Co. (Ltd.), (Montreal Star)............................	
Other companies:	
Great Northern Paper Co.......................................	197,533
Tidewater Paper Mills Co.......................................	28,798
Alexandria Paper Co..	14,971
Inland Empire Paper Co...	11,113
Nine other small companies......................................	10,709
Total..	346,865

[1] The Itasca Paper Co., Grand Rapids, Minn., was purchased by the St. Paul Dispatch and Pioneer-Press in September, 1916.

The organization of the News-Print Manufacturers Association and the concentration of control through the executive committee has led to less competition in the industry. For further information on this point see Chapter VII. This result has been aided by the existence of several selling agencies and jobbers who handle the output of various mills. For instance, as shown above, the George H. Mead Co. in 1916 handled 192,507 tons of Canadian paper. H. G. Craig & Co., another selling agency, in 1916 represented 9 different mills, being the exclusive agent of several of them. The aggregate tonnage thus concentrated amounted to more than 100,000 tons. The Manufacturers Paper Co. also sold the output of several mills. Neither of these last two concerns is directly represented on the executive committee of the News-Print Manufacturers Association.

In 1916 there was formed the Canadian Export Paper Co., the purpose of which was to pool the export business of several Canadian companies.[1] This group will be represented on the executive committee by the Laurentide officer, at present on the committee, and will probably control one-third of the entire Canadian output of news-print paper.

Section 6. Paper jobbers and sales agents.

There are two kinds of middle men handling news print—jobbers and sales agents. The distinction between the two is that the jobber usually buys and resells, while the sales agent chiefly sells on commission. The three largest sales agents on the North American continent are the George H. Mead Co., Canadian Export Paper Co., and H. G. Craig & Co. Each of these concerns represents several mills, and together they handle several hundred thousand tons of news-print paper annually. Their sales are largely to the daily papers and jobbing trade. There are several other sales agents which handle the output of a particular mill, such as W. H. Parsons & Co., which sells for the Pejepscot Paper Co., both the manufacturing and the selling company being controlled by the same interests.

The jobber handles many grades of paper and often does a commission business as well as buying and reselling on his own account. The commission business is usually for sales of news-print and book paper on contracts with publishers. When such contracts are made the jobber covers them by making similar contracts, either direct or through selling agents, with the manufacturer, who makes shipments direct to the publisher.

Almost every city of any importance has one or more jobbers or wholesale paper houses which carry various kinds of paper. Often such a house makes a specialty of some particular grade, such as high-grade printing paper, bond paper, writing paper, kraft or wrapping paper, building paper, paper bags, twine, etc. While

---

[1] For details see Chap. VII, p. 130.

practically all the jobbers handling printing paper handle some news print, very few make a specialty of it. The reason given by a number of jobbers is that there is little or no profit in it, and they only carry it, as a grocer carries sugar, to attract trade for other kinds of paper. A few of the very large jobbers, however, do a considerable business in news print, both in rolls and sheets. Ten of them perhaps handle more than 75 per cent of all the news print sold by jobbers. None of these depend on a single mill for their supply of news, although several have allotments of a certain portion of the output of a particular mill.

A considerable proportion of the sales of news print by jobbers is for miscellaneous purposes, many of them selling very little, if any, to publishers. The jobbers making a specialty of news print in addition to their contract business handle large quantities of both roll and sheet news on current transactions. Part of this business passes through the jobbers' warehouses, especially purchases in ton lots or less. Carload shipments are usually made direct from the mill. Lots from a ton up to a carload may be shipped either direct from the mill or from the jobbers' warehouses.

The principal advantage a publisher has in buying his requirements of news print through a jobber instead of direct from the manufacturer is in the matter of service. The jobber normally carries a stock of roll and sheet news, and, being more conveniently located with respect to shipping facilities than the manufacturer, can tide the publisher over in case of a sudden shortage due to such causes as failure of a car to arrive promptly, freight embargo or congestion, strikes, fires, etc. This is especially true of publishers not located in the large cities where the manufacturers keep stocks. Another advantage is in the matter of extension of credits. A customer with a good credit standing can usually secure from the jobber extensions of credit, especially if he is an old customer, whereas purchases direct from the manufacturer are usually cash or net 30 days. A third advantage for less-than-carload lots is the saving in freight. The jobber pays the carload rates for the long haul on his warehouse stock and the less-than-carload rate is charged only for the short haul.

Section 7. Imports and exports of news-print paper.

IMPORTS.—In 1901 the United States imported less than a thousand dollars worth of news print. In the fiscal year 1906 such imports amounted to only $64,382. Since that year the increase has been rapid and uninterrupted. In the fiscal year 1910 the quantity imported was twenty-five times what it had been in 1906.[1] In the calendar year 1916 the output of domestic mills supplied only about 70 per cent of the total consumption, practically all the remainder being imported from Canada.

The steadily increasing dependence of the United States on Canada for supplies of news print is shown by the following table:

TABLE 4.—IMPORTS INTO THE UNITED STATES OF PRINTING PAPER VALUED AT NOT ABOVE 2.5 CENTS[1] PER POUND, 1911–1916.

	Canada.		Total	
	Quantity.	Value.[2]	Quantity.	Value.[2]
Fiscal year ending June 30—	Tons.		Tons.	
1911	53,118	$1,968,385	54,022	$2,010,592
1912	55,563	2,101,023	56,854	2,155,501
1913	146,733	5,646,289	147,479	5,681,109
1914	274,842	10,634,926	278,071	10,765,108
1915	329,314	12,742,743	332,782	12,883,452
1916	438,212	16,646,891	438,746	16,670,604
Six months ending—				
June 30, 1915	165,644	6,418,291	166,842	6,467,864
Dec. 31, 1915	201,276	7,657,843	201,567	7,670,787
Twelve months, 1915	366,920	14,076,134	368,409	14,138,651
Six months ending—				
June 30, 1916	236,935	8,989,048	237,179	8,999,817
Dec. 31, 1916	231,017	9,625,109	231,051	9,527,931
Twelve months, 1916	467,952	18,514,157	468,230	18,527,748
Monthly:				
July, 1916	40,106	1,534,795	40,106	1,534,795
August, 1916	40,806	1,625,010	40,806	1,625,010
September, 1916	36,360	1,491,007	36,360	1,491,007
October, 1916	38,562	1,614,178	38,562	1,614,178
November, 1916	38,737	1,655,815	38,737	1,655,815
December, 1916	36,446	1,604,304	36,480	1,607,126

[1] Since Sept. 8, 1916, 5 cents per pound.
[2] These figures do not represent accurately the cost of this news print to the American publisher as most of the paper is entered at an officially established valuation of $38 per ton.

Fiscal year imports increased from 54,022 tons in 1911 to 438,746 tons in 1916. Since 1912 the annual increase has not fallen below 50,000 tons, and in two years it has exceeded 100,000 tons. In the fiscal year 1916 these imports were over eight times as large as in 1911. They increased from 368,409 tons in the calendar year 1915 to 468,230 tons in 1916.

[1] Import statistics never have carried a news-print classification, and the classification by value, used here, was shown only under " Imports for consumption " prior to 1911. Since that date it is also shown in the regular import returns.

Canada's rapid progress as a factor in the situation is illustrated by the increase in the proportion of the total supply of the United States imported from that country. Ten years ago Canada furnished but a fraction of 1 per cent of the news print used in the United States; in 1909, less than 4 per cent; in 1916, about 30 per cent. The imports from Canada amounted to about 75 per cent of the total Canadian production in the calendar year 1915 and about 78 per cent in 1916. In the latter year Canada's over-sea exports amounted to about 53,000 tons, or 9 per cent of the total output, leaving about 81,800 tons or 13 per cent for home consumption.

A very large part of the imports from Canada come in over the northern border, but since 1913 entries at Pacific ports have usually run from one to one and a half million dollars annually. These figures, of course, take no account of the exchange arrangement between a United States and Canadian company referred to on page 47 below.

IMPORT DUTIES.—For 124 years prior to 1913 duties were imposed upon the importation of news-print paper into the United States. The tariff law passed in 1909 reduced the duty to three-sixteenths of a cent per pound, equivalent to $3.75 a ton, upon news print valued at not above $2\frac{1}{4}$ cents per pound, and the Canadian reciprocity law passed in 1911 removed the duty entirely on imports of news-print paper and pulp from Canada, except where the Canadian Government imposed an export duty. The tariff act of 1913 put news-print paper from all countries valued at not above $2\frac{1}{2}$ cents per pound upon the free list. If valued at above $2\frac{1}{2}$ cents per pound a duty of 12 per cent was imposed. About 60 per cent of the Canadian paper came in free in 1912. In 1913 over $1,000,000 worth of the Canadian paper was still paying duty, but since October 3, 1913, no duty has been paid on printing paper valued at not over $2\frac{1}{2}$ cents per pound in the country whence exported. The rise in price in 1916 led to the enactment of a provision in the revenue law approved September 8, 1916, raising the minimum of $2\frac{1}{4}$ cents per pound to 5 cents. This was done in anticipation of the market price in Canada going above $2\frac{1}{4}$ cents, which would cause the 12 per cent duty to be imposed upon imports into this country. For further details see Exhibits 3 and 4.

EXPORTS.—Prior to 1911 export figures were not shown separately in our foreign-trade statistics. Since 1911 they have run as Table 5 indicates:

TABLE 5.—EXPORTS OF NEWS-PRINT PAPER FROM THE UNITED STATES, 1911–1916.

Periods.	Quantity.	Total value.	Value per ton.
Fiscal year ending June 30—	*Tons.*		
1911	49,755	$2,434,964	$48.92
1912	51,787	2,501,529	48.30
1913	50,213	2,450,520	48.80
1914	44,483	2,177,483	48.91
1915	62,841	3,070,137	48.98
1916	63,634	3,119,364	49.02
6 months ending—			
June 30, 1915	25,752	1,307,732	50.78
Dec. 31, 1915	29,409	1,399,894	47.60
12 months, 1915	55,161	2,707,626	49.09
6 months ending—			
June 30, 1916	34,212	1,715,917	50.16
Dec. 31, 1916	42,115	2,378,858	56.48
12 months, 1916	76,327	4,094,775	53.64
Months:			
July, 1916	7,454	422,486	56.68
August, 1916	11,636	599,354	51.51
September, 1916	6,597	370,704	56.19
October, 1916	4,941	316,061	63.97
November, 1916	5,618	311,183	55.39
December, 1916	5,870	359,070	61.17

The smallest quantity exported during the last six fiscal years was 44,483 tons in 1914 immediately preceding the outbreak of the European war. In the calendar year 1916 exports had increased to 76,327 tons, which was 5.6 per cent of the domestic production for the same period.

The increase in exports in 1916 was in considerable degree due to shipments to various countries such as France, Portugal, Greece, China, etc., which prior to the year 1916 imported little or no news print from this country.

The only domestic manufacturer that has developed an export trade of considerable importance is the International Paper Co. That company supplies foreign publishers under contracts similar to those used in the domestic trade. Aside from the International's business, news print exports are apparently made up of odd lots handled by trading companies. That there was a considerable increase in this odd lot business during 1916 is indicated by the fact that the International Paper Co.'s proportion of total exports fell from 85.6 per cent in the first half of 1915 to 61 per cent in the first half of 1916. Prior to 1915, so far as information is available, that company's proportion of the total had never fallen below 75 per cent.

The records of the Bureau of Foreign and Domestic Commerce show a considerable variation in prices on news-print paper exported during a given month. For example, shipments to Australia in August, 1916, varied from less than 2 to over 5 cents per pound. The low price which was on shipments from Portland, Oreg., was due to an exchange of paper between a Canadian and a United States company, the latter exporting for the former, in exchange for Canadian paper delivered in other Pacific coast ports. This arrangement was made because the Canadian company could not obtain shipping facilities in Vancouver or Seattle. Export figures for later months in the year indicated that this exchange arrangement was still in force. These shipments probably amounted to over 5,000 tons during 1916.

CHAPTER III.

PRICES OF NEWS-PRINT PAPER.

Section 1. Introduction.

The great bulk of the news-print paper output on the North American Continent is bought by publishers of the larger dailies on contracts which provide for the delivery of a certain tonnage at a fixed price. The contracts usually run for one year, but on the Pacific coast the prevailing term is five years. These larger publishers use roll paper, which is shipped to them in carload lots directly from the mill, though frequently purchased from a jobber or selling agent.

The large number of the smaller dailies, weeklies, and semiweeklies, which depend upon the open market for their supplies of paper, use a relatively small part of the news-print output. Most of these publishers use sheet paper, which is purchased in less than carload lots from jobbers.

The detailed price data presented herein show the open-market prices paid by the smaller publishers and the contract prices paid by the larger publishers in 1916 and prior years. To show what effect the increase in prices to publishers which occurred in 1916 had on the receipts of news-print manufacturers, the average receipts per ton f. o. b. mill have also been computed for mills in different years.

Price statistics were obtained from the original contracts on file in the offices of the various paper mills and jobbers visited by agents of the Commission, from the sales records of these companies, and from data furnished by newspaper publishers in response to schedules sent them by the Commission.

Prices paid by different publishers vary widely during the same period. These differences depend partly upon distance from mills, method of purchase, size of purchase, quality of the paper, and credit standing of the purchaser.

The chief cause of the variation in prices between different sections of the country is the wide range in freight rates due to the localization of the news-print industry in the spruce timber regions of northern United States and in Canada. The relatively high

48

freight rate on news print in comparison with its value at the mill makes this an important factor. As compared with freight rates of 12 to 15 cents per 100 pounds on carload shipments to New York City, for example, the rates on similar shipments to certain cities of the Southwest are more than $1, representing at the prevailing market price during the year 1915 approximately 30 per cent of the total cost to the purchaser. The cost to the publisher of the East, the North, and the Pacific Northwest was accordingly 15 to 25 per cent lower than the cost to purchasers in the extreme South and Southwest.

Variations in prices paid by different publishers in the same locality are due to the method of purchase, the size of purchase, and the quality of the paper. Contract purchases ordinarily average a lower price than market purchases, and transactions involving large quantities a lower price than those involving small quantities. Small purchases are made through jobbers, as a rule, and must bear middlemen's profits and commissions. Instances have been noted where paper has passed through as many as three middlemen's hands before reaching the publisher.

Even when the quantities of paper purchased are the same and the publishers are in the same locality there is a variation in prices, due to the fact that some of the mills are able to get a higher price than others on account of the quality of their paper, greater ability to deliver on their contracts, etc.

The price statistics have been assembled as far as possible in a manner to bring out the effect of the various factors which govern the price of news print in different localities and among different classes of purchasers. This has involved a separation of contract prices from market or current prices, and the grouping of the data by quantity sold, and by localities having the same general level of freight rates.

In order to facilitate a comparison by localities the country has been divided into six groups of States, as follows:

(1) *Eastern.*—This group includes the New England States and the States of New York and New Jersey, Delaware, Pennsylvania, Maryland and Virginia. The news-print paper consumed in these States is a product of the mills of the eastern United States and Canada. Freight charges on paper shipped in carload lots from Canada average about 20 cents per 100 pounds to localities north of the Potomac River as compared with about 30 cents to Virginia. In the case of shipments from domestic mills the freight rate on carload lots is about 14 cents to New York City as against about 17 cents to localities in Pennsylvania and about 20 cents to points in Virginia.

(2) *Middle Western.*--This group includes the States of West Virginia, Ohio, Indiana, Illinois, and Kentucky. News-print paper used in this territory is obtained in some cases from centers of production in the eastern United States and Canada, but to a large extent is the product of the paper mills in the States bordering on the Great Lakes and the adjoining Canadian Province. Within this group freight rates on carload lots vary from about 10 to 20 cents to points in Ohio and northern Illinois and Indiana, with an average of about 20 cents to points in West Virginia and Kentucky.

(3) *Southern.*--This group includes the territory south of Virginia and Kentucky and east of the Mississippi River. The news print consumed in this territory is largely the product of the paper mills of New England and the States bordering on the Great Lakes, and, in the case of the smaller papers, is usually purchased from jobbers in the South and Middle West. The freight rates per 100 pounds on news print shipped in carload quantities to cities within this group range from a minimum of about 26 cents to a maximum of about 45 cents.

(4) *North Central.*--This group includes the States of Michigan, Wisconsin, and Minnesota, each of which contains one or more news-print mills. The freight rate on paper consumed within this group is relatively low, averaging about 13 cents per 100 pounds in the case of carload shipments from domestic mills. On shipments from Canadian mills the freight rates average about 18 cents.

(5) *Western.*--This group includes the territory between the Mississippi River and the States of the Pacific coast, with the exception of Minnesota. News-print paper sold in this territory is drawn from as far east as the Province of Quebec, Canada, and as far west as British Columbia. On account of the distance from the centers of production, the price of paper in this territory is relatively high. The freight rates on carload shipments range from about 15 cents on deliveries in Iowa to $1.07 on shipments to localities near the southwestern border of the United States.

(6) *Pacific coast.*--The States of California, Oregon, and Washington are included in this group. Most of the important daily papers in these States obtain news-print paper under contracts with mills in the Pacific Northwest. The newspapers of smaller circulation purchase paper, as a rule, through jobbers in Seattle, Portland, Los Angeles, and San Francisco. Contract prices in this group show a wide variation. The range in freight charges on carload shipments is from a rate of about 7.5 cents in Oregon to a rate of about 62.5 cents to southern California.

Section 2. Open-market prices.

There was a large increase in prices paid by publishers purchasing their paper on current orders as needed during 1916. This increase was much greater than for contract purchases, which are considered later. Only a small proportion of the total sales of news-print paper, probably not more than 10 per cent, is sold on current orders. Under ordinary conditions most of this is sheet paper which is bought in small quantities by country weeklies, while some of it is roll paper bought by publishers of small dailies whose requirements do not amount to more than a car or two a year. During 1916, however, considerable quantities of roll paper were purchased in the open market by publishers of the larger dailies whose contracts did not cover their entire requirements on account of increased consumption, or who were unable to renew their contracts.

The open-market prices of roll paper in carload lots or over in 1915 were generally less than $2.35 per 100 pounds f. o. b. destination, while during the third quarter of 1916 the minimum prices in practically all the States for which prices were tabulated were more than $3, and by December, 1916, the price had advanced to more than $5 f. o. b. mill.

Open-market prices for sheet news showed an even greater increase in 1916. For current orders of from 1 to 17 tons, inclusive, the maximum prices in the third quarter of 1916 were in many cases higher by $2 to $3 per 100 pounds than the maximum prices in 1915, while in December, 1916, the prices were sometimes $4 per 100 pounds higher than in 1915.

RANGE OF OPEN-MARKET PRICES OF ROLL NEWS.—Table 6 below shows the range in prices paid by publishers on market purchases of not less than one car, or 18 tons of news-print paper in rolls, for the year 1915 and for each of the first three quarters of 1916. Owing to lack of time it was impossible for the Commission to obtain complete data for the third quarter of 1916 from all of the companies represented in the tabulation for the earlier periods. The figures for this quarter should therefore be accepted with caution. Information received from publishers shows that sales were made in a number of instances during the third quarter of 1916 at materially higher prices than are shown in the table.

TABLE 6.—RANGE OF OPEN-MARKET PRICES TO PUBLISHERS ON PURCHASES OF 12 TONS OR OVER, OF NEWS-PRINT PAPER IN ROLLS, BY STATES, 1915-1916.

[Delivered f. o. b. destination.]

Group and State.	Date of order and range of prices per 100 pounds.			
	1915	1916		
		First quarter.	Second quarter.	Third quarter.[1]
Eastern group:				
Massachusetts	$2.10-$2.35	$2.10-$2.35		$3.21-$3.91
Rhode Island and Connecticut				3.41- 3.51
New York	1.98- 2.61	2.10- 2.80	$2.55-$3.50	2.75- 3.55
New Jersey	2.05- 2.35	2.20- 2.50	2.41	
Pennsylvania	2.00- 2.25	2.00- 2.35	2.20- 3.50	2.23- 4.25
Middle Western group:				
West Virginia	2.02- 2.15	2.15- 2.35	2.30- 3.50	3.75
Ohio	1.92- 2.15	1.92- 2.39	2.05- 3.37	
Indiana	2.05- 2.25	2.00- 2.44	2.02- 3.50	3.50- 3.80
Illinois	1.94- 2.41	2.00- 2.50	3.14- 4.00	3.14- 4.50
Kentucky	2.04- 2.18	2.13- 2.49	3.50- 4.00	3.27- 3.49
North Central group:				
Michigan, Wisconsin, and Minnesota	1.95- 2.15	2.11- 2.28	2.23- 3.75	4.83- 5.00
Western group:				
Iowa	2.10- 2.21	2.15- 2.49	2.50- 3.49	
South Dakota	2.32		4.02	
Nebraska and Kansas		2.33- 2.35	2.25- 4.20	4.00- 5.36
Missouri and Arkansas	2.00- 2.52	2.75	3.60	

[1] Prices for the third quarter are not complete, especially for September.

Comparing the year 1915 with the third quarter of 1916, the greatest increases in prices, as shown by the ranges in the table, were as follows: Michigan, Wisconsin, and Minnesota, from a range of $1.95-$2.15 to $4.83-$5 per 100 pounds; Indiana, from a range of $2.05-$2.25 to a range of $3.50-$3.80 per 100 pounds; Massachusetts, from a range of $2.10-$2.35 to a range of $3.21-$3.91; Kentucky, from a range of $2.04-$2.18 to a range of $3.27-$3.49; and Pennsylvania, from a range of $2-$2.25 to a range of $2.23-$4.25.

During the last quarter of 1916 open-market prices continued to advance. In December, 1916, roll news frequently ranged from $5 to $6 per 100 pounds f. o. b. mill as compared with a range of $1.92 to $2.61 per 100 pounds f. o. b. destination in 1915.

RANGE OF OPEN-MARKET PRICES OF SHEET NEWS.—The price of newsprint paper in sheets is influenced by a number of factors which tend to increase the cost to the consumer above the price level of roll paper. The cost of manufacture of paper in sheets is somewhat greater than in rolls owing to the additional labor involved in its preparation for market. The f. o. b. mill price, as a rule, is from 10 cents to 20 cents more per 100 pounds for sheet paper than for rolls.

Paper finished in sheets usually reaches the consumer through job-bers, and is delivered in less-than-carload quantities to a much greater extent than roll paper. Freight and jobbers' profits are ac-cordingly higher as a whole on sheet paper than on roll paper.

Table 7 below shows the course of market prices paid by publishers for sheet news in quantities varying from 1 to 17 tons, inclusive, for the year 1915 and for each of the first three quarters of 1916. The figures given for the third quarter of 1916 represent only a small percentage of the total sales and are not fully representative of price fluctuations during that period.

TABLE 7.—RANGE OF OPEN-MARKET PRICES TO PUBLISHERS ON PURCHASES OF 1 TO 17 TONS, INCLUSIVE, OF NEWS-PRINT PAPER IN SHEETS, BY STATES, 1915-1916.

[Deliveries f. o. b. destination.]

| | Date of order and range of prices per 100 pounds. | | | |
| | | 1916 | | |
Group and State.	1915	First quarter.	Second quarter.	Third quarter.[1]
Eastern group:				
Maine and New Hampshire..................	$2.40-$2.75	$2.40-$2.75	$2.75-$3.50	$3.40-$4.65
Massachusetts and Connecticut.............	2.18- 3.50	2.45- 3.75	3.00- 4.50	3.02- 6.00
New York..............................	2.08- 3.00	2.20- 3.05	2.35- 5.00	3.39- 5.50
New Jersey.............................	2.20- 3.30	2.35- 3.60	2.35- 4.10	3.66- 5.25
Pennsylvania...........................	2.15- 3.00	2.45- 4.50	2.75- 4.50	3.66- 6.00
Delaware and Maryland..................	2.35- 2.75	2.75- 3.41	3.21	4.50
Middle Western group:				
West Virginia..........................	2.10- 2.60	2.35- 2.85	2.75- 4.95	4.00- 5.60
Ohio.................................	2.30- 2.70	2.45- 3.25	3.00- 4.15	4.60- 6.46
Indiana...............................	2.15- 2.80	2.26- 3.50	2.60- 4.00	3.25- 5.59
Kentucky.............................	2.35- 3.10	2.60	2.60- 4.50	4.50- 5.60
Illinois...............................	2.20- 2.95	2.34- 3.50	2.63- 5.00	4.22- 6.09
North Central group:				
Michigan..............................	2.05- 3.00	2.25- 3.00	2.53- 4.65	3.65- 4.75
Wisconsin.............................	2.10- 2.85	2.40- 3.00	2.75- 4.45	5.50- 6.00
Minnesota............................	2.30- 2.75	2.40- 3.00	2.55- 4.50	4.00- 5.75
Southern group:				
North Carolina........................	2.35- 2.65	2.50- 3.25	3.25- 4.50	3.50
South Carolina........................	2.30- 3.15	2.50- 3.25	2.55- 4.00	3.84- 4.20
Georgia..............................	2.40- 2.75	2.40- 3.00	2.95- 4.25	3.90- 4.50
Tennessee............................	2.60- 2.90	2.25- 3.75	3.75- 4.40	4.70
Alabama..............................	2.40- 2.50	2.55- 2.85	2.70- 4.63	5.00
Florida...............................	3.50- 3.75	4.00	4.00- 4.50	....
Mississippi............................	2.30- 2.65	2.50- 4.00	3.00- 4.00	4.00- 4.50
Western group:				
Iowa.................................	2.20- 3.00	2.37- 3.20	2.40- 4.50	4.70- 6.00
Missouri..............................	2.30- 2.90	2.17- 4.15	3.32- 4.65	4.43- 6.07
North Dakota..........................	2.40- 2.93	2.50- 3.50	3.25- 4.75	5.00- 5.28
South Dakota..........................	2.65- 2.86	2.70- 3.25	3.25- 4.51	....
Nebraska..............................	2.52- 2.95	2.18	4.00- 4.95	3.83- 6.75
Kansas...............................	2.50- 3.10	2.50- 4.15	3.15- 5.05	4.25- 6.25

[1] Prices for the third quarter of 1916 are not complete, especially for September.

TABLE 7.—RANGE OF OPEN-MARKET PRICES TO PUBLISHERS ON PURCHASES OF 1 TO
17 TONS, INCLUSIVE OF NEWS-PRINT PAPER IN SHEETS, ETC.—Continued.

| | Date of order and range of prices per 100 pounds. | | | |
| | | 1916 | | |
Group and State.	1915	First quarter.	Second quarter.	Third quarter.
Western group continued.				
Idaho...	$3.60	$3.50	....	$4.75-$5.00
Oklahoma..	$2.95- 3.10	$2.95- 3.55	$3.60-$4.50	4.50- 5.50
Montana..	2.50- 3.81	3.15- 3.91	3.91- 5.75	4.60- 6.25
Texas...	2.55- 3.15	3.00- 3.50	3.25- 5.00	5.00- 7.00
Utah..	3.75	3.75	....	4.50- 5.29
New Mexico and Arizona.....................	3.25- 4.10	3.25- 3.75	3.25- 4.65	5.00- 5.75
Pacific coast group:				
Washington......................................	3.00- 4.14	3.15- 4.50	3.50- 4.93	4.00- 6.14
Oregon...	2.70- 4.04	3.10- 4.18	3.64- 4.85	4.50- 5.58
California..	2.60- 4.50	2.84- 4.50	3.25- 6.50	3.25- 6.00

This table shows that there was a rapid increase in prices on orders
of from 1 to 17 tons of news-print paper in sheets during 1916. In
fact, the minimum prices were higher in all but two States—Washington and California—during the third quarter of 1916 than the maximum prices of 1915. In many cases they were more than $1 per 100
pounds higher. The maximum prices in the third quarter of 1916
were in many cases higher by $2 to $3 or more per 100 pounds than
the maximum prices in 1915.

The greatest increase in the general level of prices, as indicated by
the ranges, was in the western group, which includes the States west
of the Mississippi River, except the Pacific coast group, while the
smallest increase was found in the latter group.

In the last quarter of 1916 open-market prices on sheet news continued to advance. In December, 1916, prices for less-than-carload
lots often ranged from $6.50 to $7.50 per 100 pounds, as compared with
$2.20 to $4.20 at the beginning of the year. In some cases sheet paper
in less than ton lots sold for $8 or more per 100 pounds.

During the latter part of February, 1917, the open-market price
on sheet news in ton lots decreased to a range of from about $5 to $7
per 100 pounds. For jobbers' sales prices of roll and sheet news see
pages 78 and 79.

PRICES OF READY-PRINT SHEETS.—More than 90 per cent of the ready
print used in the United States is furnished by the Western Newspaper Union. The price of ready print varies according to the size of
sheet and quantity purchased and whether with or without advertising. It is issued in folios (two pages printed and two pages blank)
and in quartos (four pages printed and four pages blank). The six-

column quarto, size 30½ by 44—50-pound paper, is the one most used. The prices of the Western Newspaper Union for this size of ready print from August 1, 1913, to August 1, 1916, inclusive, are shown in the table below:

TABLE 8.—PRICES OF THE WESTERN NEWSPAPER UNION FOR READY-PRINT SHEETS PER QUIRE OF SIX-COLUMN QUARTO, 30½ BY 44—50-POUND PAPER, AUG. 1, 1913, TO AUG. 1, 1916, INCLUSIVE.

[Eight pages, four printed and four blank.]

Quantity.	Aug. 1, 1913, to July 31, 1916.		Effective from Aug. 1, 1916.	
	With advertising.	Without advertising.	With advertising.	Without advertising.
Under 20 quires..	$0.14	$0.22	$0.17	$0.25
20 to 29 quires..	.13	.21	.16	.24
30 to 39 quires..	.12	.20	.15	.23
40 to 49 quires..	.11	.19	.14	.22
50 to 59 quires..	.10	.18	.13	.21
60 quires and over..	.09	.17	.12	.20

These prices are f. o. b. the nearest branch office of the Western Newspaper Union. About 97 per cent of the papers supplied by this company use ready print with advertising already printed on it.

There was no change in prices between August 1, 1913, and July 31, 1916, while the increase, effective August 1, 1916, was 3 cents per quire. On paper with advertising this amounted to an increase of from 21.4 to 33.3 per cent, according to the quantity ordered.

A circular letter to ready-print customers guaranteed that the rates effective August 1, 1916, would not be increased during the next 12 months, and that when market conditions become normal and former paper prices are restored the rates will be reduced accordingly.

Section 3. Contract prices.

There was a slight decrease in the prices at which contracts for news-print paper were made during the period from 1912 to 1915, inclusive. There was a continuous increase, however, in the prices on contracts made during 1916. On most of the tonnage contracted for during the latter part of 1916 this increase was about 60 per cent. In some cases the increase was more than 100 per cent.

About 90 per cent of the total shipments of news-print paper is sold under contract. Most of this is roll paper and is used by daily papers. Most of the daily papers in the larger cities use more than 1,000 tons of paper per year. In some cases they use as high as 30,000 tons or over. On the other hand, the daily papers in the smaller cities ordinarily use less than 1,000 tons per year, and in many cases 100 tons or less.

PROVISIONS OF CONTRACTS.—Daily papers obtain news print as a rule under contracts direct with manufacturers or through large wholesale companies, which provide for the delivery to the purchaser of a certain tonnage of paper at the price, on the terms, and for the period stipulated in the agreement.[1]

Three common forms of tonnage specifications existed prior to 1917: (1) provision for the entire supply with an estimate of the tonnage required; (2) a maximum and minimum tonnage specified; and (3) a given tonnage specified, with a leeway of from 5 to 10 per cent. The present standard contracts provide for a fixed tonnage.

In the territory east of the Mississippi River comparatively few of the existing contracts cover a period of more than one year, and in some recent cases they are limited to shorter periods, while on the Pacific coast contracts with the larger dailies usually cover a period of five years. Where contracts were made shortly after the inception of the upward trend in prices, they were in some instances limited to a period of not more than six months. Most of the contracts made to begin during the last half of 1916 were drawn to expire with the end of the calendar year. Some of the contracts which expired during that period were not renewed, the publishers being placed on a current market basis.

The prices paid by publishers for news-print paper in some cases include the cost of delivery at the city of publication, and in others are f. o. b. mill, transportation charges being collected from the customer by the transportation agencies. In contracts between news-print manufacturers and the large metropolitan dailies the price, until recent months, has usually been for delivery at the pressroom of the publisher, the payment of both freight and drayage charges being assumed by the manufacturer. As a measure of protection to the purchaser in the case of an interruption of traffic, such contracts have usually contained a stipulation requiring the manufacturer to keep in storage at all times in the city at which the paper is delivered a sufficient quantity to meet the requirements of the publisher for a specified period, usually not less than 10 days to 2 weeks' requirements.

In connection with the marked advance in the price of news-print paper in 1916, a new policy was announced by many news-print paper manufacturers in both the United States and Canada, namely, the discontinuance of sales for delivery at the pressroom or railroad delivery station and a substitution of delivery to the purchaser at the mill. This policy was reflected in the sales records of a number of the large eastern mills for the months of July and August, 1916, and has been adopted in almost all of the contracts made since then. By selling f. o. b. mill, instead of sidewalk or pressroom, the man-

---

[1] See Exhibit 5 for forms of contract.

ufacturer is relieved of the necessity of carrying a supply of paper in storage in various cities in which his customers are located, of providing cartage facilities for sidewalk delivery, and also of the trouble of collecting damages from the railroads for injury to the paper in transit. Any increase in the freight rates and cartage charges must now be borne by the publisher.

In the territory north of the Potomac and Ohio Rivers and east of the Missouri River the freight rates to most points range between 7.5 and 25 cents per 100 pounds with an average of about 15 cents. South of the Potomac and Ohio Rivers and east of the Mississippi River the freight rates range between 20 and 45 cents per 100 pounds. In the Southwest the rates range from 40 cents to over $1 per 100 pounds.

In 1916 the cartage charges in various cities ranged from 2.5 cents to 5 cents per 100 pounds, and storage charges, in cases where the paper was stored, were about 2.5 cents additional. Cartage and storage together generally amounted to about 5 cents per 100 pounds, although in some cases they were as high as 8 or 9 cents per 100 pounds. However, the individual publishers are now paying higher cartage and storage charges than were paid by the manufacturers in 1916 for deliveries to the same publishers.

All new taxes that may be levied upon news-print paper are also to be paid by the publisher. The contract form of one large manufacturing company contains the following clause on this point:

> Any new tax of any nature which may hereafter be levied by any Government, State, or municipality increasing the cost of all or any portion of the said paper or any of the materials used in the manufacture thereof shall be added to the said price to be paid by the purchaser.

No leeway is allowed in the tonnage. The publisher must order a definite tonnage to be taken during the contract period in equal monthly installments, although the consumption varies at different seasons of the year.

It is clear that these changes in the terms of contracts must increase the actual cost of the paper to publishers. A traffic specialist employed by a great manufacturing corporation is in position to reduce actual costs of transportation and minimize the chances of damage in transit. A single stock in any one locality from which a number of publishers draw their supplies does not need to be nearly so large as the aggregate of the stocks that are necessary if each publisher stores his own reserves.

These and other similar additions to the burden of the publishers under the present form of contract together constitute an economic loss to the country as a whole, which will be found to be very considerable in amount.

RANGE OF PRICES ON CONTRACTS FOR 1,000 TONS OR OVER.—In the following table is shown the course of prices from 1912 to 1916 in 32 large cities on contracts involving not less than 1,000 tons of paper. The figures include the highest and lowest prices on contracts made in each period for paper delivered in the city of publication, either at the railroad station or on the sidewalk at the pressroom of the publisher. In the case of contracts based on delivery at the mill, destination prices were obtained by adding to the mill price the freight rate to destination. Where this rate was not shown by the records of the jobber or manufacturer, rates were obtained from tariffs filed with the Interstate Commerce Commission. The sidewalk prices differ from destination prices by the inclusion in the former of drayage and storage charges, which range from 2.5 to 5 cents per 100 pounds.

TABLE 9.—RANGE OF PRICES ON CONTRACTS WITH PUBLISHERS FOR 1,000 TONS OR OVER OF NEWS-PRINT PAPER IN ROLLS, BY CITIES, 1912-1916 (FIRST HALF).

Group and city.	Delivery on sidewalk or f. o. b. car, destination.	Date of signing contract and range of prices in dollars per 100 pounds.				1916	
		1912	1913	1914	1915	January-March.	April-June.
Eastern group:							
Boston, Mass.	Sidewalk	$2.03-$2.30	$2.05-$2.25	$2.00-$2.20	$2.02-$2.15	$2.18	$2.25
Albany, N. Y.	...do...		¹2.04- 2.15	¹2.01- 2.15	2.00- 2.15		
Buffalo, N. Y.	...do...	2.10	2.00- 2.10	2.00- 2.20	2.00- 2.10	¹2.14	
Rochester, N. Y.	...do...		2.00- 2.11	2.10-¹2.21	2.05- 2.13	2.13	
Syracuse, N. Y.	...do...	¹2.12	2.02	¹2.09- 2.10	1.98- 2.02		
New York, N. Y.	...do...	2.07- 2.25	2.05- 2.25	2.05- 2.20	2.00- 2.20	$2.07- 2.15	
Newark, N. J.	Destination	2.15	2.05- 2.10	2.10-¹2.11	2.05-²2.00		
Philadelphia, Pa.	Sidewalk	2.12- 2.25	2.03- 2.25	2.05- 2.18	2.08- 2.18	2.10- 2.15	²2.08
Pittsburgh, Pa.	...do...	2.12- 2.25	2.15- 2.25	2.00- 2.15	2.00- 2.15	2.10- 2.15	
Scranton, Pa.	...do...			2.05	2.05- 2.10	2.13	2.34
Washington, D. C.	...do...	2.16- 2.25	2.15	2.10- 2.15	2.15	2.18	
Richmond, Va.	...do...	¹2.29	2.15-¹2.19	2.09-¹2.19	2.10		2.54
Middle Western group:							
Cleveland, Ohio	...do...	2.15- 2.25	2.08- 2.10	2.05- 2.10	1.07- 2.02		2.22
Columbus, Ohio	...do...	¹2.15- 2.25	¹2.05- 2.10	¹2.02- 2.10	2.05-¹2.06	¹2.03	2.45
Dayton, Ohio	...do...	2.25	2.10- 2.15		2.15	2.00- 2.05	
Toledo, Ohio	Destination	¹2.21	2.05	2.03- 2.10	1.99- 2.10		2.40
Cincinnati, Ohio	Sidewalk	2.20- 2.25	2.10- 2.15	2.06- 2.17	¹2.04- 2.15		¹2.44
Indianapolis, Ind.	...do...	2.16	2.09- 2.13	¹2.09-¹2.14	2.07-¹2.11		
Louisville, Ky.	...do...	2.25	2.09- 2.15	2.05- 2.17	2.12- 2.15	2.22	2.35
Chicago, Ill.	...do...	2.09- 2.25	2.05- 2.25	2.03- 2.15	1.99- 2.05	¹2.14	¹2.74

[1]Cartage charges estimated at 4 cents per 100 pounds added to gross selling price.
[2]Cartage charges estimated at 4 cents per 100 pounds deducted from gross selling price.
[3]Executed in May, 1916, but effective as of Jan. 1, 1916.

TABLE 9.—RANGE OF PRICES ON CONTRACTS WITH PUBLISHERS FOR 1,000 TONS OR OVER OF NEWS-PRINT PAPER IN ROLLS, BY CITIES, 1912-1916 (FIRST HALF)—Continued.

Group and city.	Delivery on side-walk or f. o. b. car, designation.	Date of signing contract and range of prices in dollars per 100 pounds.				1916	
		1912	1913	1914	1915	January-March.	April-June.
North Central Group:							
Detroit, Mich	Sidewalk	$2.25	$2.08- 2.09	$2.05- 2.12	$2.04- 2.05	¹ $2.25	....
Milwaukee, Wis	Destination	$2.05- 2.10	2.05- 2.27	2.05- 2.08	1.95- 2.10	2.08	$2.30
Minneapolis, Minn	do	2.22	2.07	2.00- 2.07	2.00- 2.07	....	2.40
St. Paul, Minn	do	2.05	2.01	2.01	2.01	....	2.40
Southern group:							
Memphis, Tenn	Sidewalk	....	2.17- 2.25	2.15- 2.22	2.13- 2.21	....	2.50
Nashville, Tenn	Destination	2.30	2.18- 2.30	2.18- 2.25	2.10	....	....
Atlanta, Ga	do	2.29- 2.35	2.25- 2.35	2.35	2.29- 2.35	....	....
Birmingham, Ala	do	2.40- 2.41	2.20- 2.35	2.19-² 2.31	2.27- 2.40	2.40	2.40
New Orleans, La	do	2.18- 2.25	2.18- 2.33	2.25- 2.28	2.21- 2.25	2.40	2.58
Western group:							
Kansas City, Mo	do	² 2.10- 2.25	2.12- 2.20	2.10- 2.12	2.10- 2.11	....	$2.49- 2.51
Omaha, Nebr	do	2.20	2.20	2.03- 2.19	1.98- 2.16	2.26	2.40
Denver, Colo	do	....	2.54	2.38- 2.54	2.36- 2.49	2.53	2.73- 2.83

¹ Cartage charges estimated at 4 cents per 100 pounds added to gross selling price.
² Cartage charges estimated at 4 cents per 100 pounds deducted from gross selling price.

The above table shows that the prices of news-print paper on contracts of 1,000 tons or over decreased slightly from 1912 to 1915. This was true in most cases for both the lowest and highest prices. Relatively few contracts were made during the first six months of 1916.

In the first quarter of 1916 the general level of contract prices was somewhat higher than in 1915, there being few cities in which there were prices as low as the minimum prices in 1915, while in a number of cities there were prices higher than the maximum prices in 1915.

In the second quarter of 1916 there was a distinct advance over the maximum prices of 1915, except in a few cities. The most notable advances in maximum prices were in the following cities: Chicago, Ill., from $2.05 to $2.74, an advance of 69 cents per 100 pounds; Richmond, Va., from $2.10 to $2.54, an advance of 44 cents; Kansas City, Mo., from $2.11 to $2.51, an advance of 40 cents; Columbus, Ohio, from $2.06 to $2.45, an advance of 39 cents; St. Paul, Minn., from $2.01 to $2.40, an advance of 39 cents; Denver, Colo., from $2.49 to $2.83, an advance of 34 cents; Minneapolis, Minn., from $2.07 to $2.40, an advance of 33 cents; New Orleans, La., from $2.25 to $2.58, an advance of 33 cents; and Toledo, Ohio, from $2.10 to $2.40, an advance of 30 cents. It will be noted that all these cities are south of the Potomac or west of the Appalachian Mountains. There were also advances in maximum prices ranging from 20 to 29 cents per 100 pounds in Cincinnati, Ohio; Memphis, Tenn.; Omaha, Nebr.; Scranton, Pa.; Cleveland, Ohio; Milwaukee, Wis.; and Louisville, Ky. Scranton, Pa., is the only one of these cities north of the Potomac and east of the Alleghenies.

In a number of the cities no contracts were signed during the second quarter of 1916, while in a few others contracts were signed at about the same level as the 1915 prices. Examples of the latter are Boston, Mass.; Philadelphia, Pa.; and Birmingham, Ala. The Boston price was on a contract signed in April, 1916. The Philadelphia price was on a contract which, although signed in May, 1916, was effective as of January 1, 1916.

Only one contract involving 1,000 tons or more of news print was made in the Pacific coast group in 1916. As prices for the period 1912 to 1915 alone would have no material significance, they have not been included in the table.

RANGE OF PRICES ON CONTRACTS FOR 100 TO 999 TONS.—Table 10 following gives the range in prices on contracts for 100 to 999 tons, inclusive, of news print in rolls, by States, for the years 1913 to 1915 and for each of the first two quarters of 1916.

TABLE 10.—RANGE OF PRICES ON CONTRACTS WITH PUBLISHERS FOR 100 TO 999 TONS, INCLUSIVE, OF NEWS-PRINT PAPER IN ROLLS, BY STATES, 1913–1916 (FIRST HALF).

[Deliveries f. o. b. destination.]

Group and State.	Date of signing contract and range of prices per 100 pounds.				
	1913	1914	1915	1916	
				January–March.	April–June.
Eastern group:					
New Hampshire and Vermont...................	$2.05–$2.35	$2.02–$2.25	$1.97–$2.25	$2.17–$2.30	$2.37
Massachusetts, Rhode Island, and Connecticut..........	1.95– 2.31	1.96– 2.35	1.96– 2.21	2.15– 2.31	$2.30– 2.61
New York and New Jersey..	1.96– 2.35	2.00– 2.41	1.98– 2.35	2.10– 2.31	2.09– 3.27
Pennsylvania, Delaware, and Maryland.................	1.98– 2.30	1.98– 2.30	1.98– 2.30	2.05– 2.18	2.03– 3.16
Virginia...................	2.06– 2.20	2.04– 2.28	2.06– 2.26	2.28	2.34
Middle Western group:					
West Virginia...............	2.05	2.05– 2.15	2.03– 2.19	....	2.50
Ohio and Indiana............	2.00– 2.35	1.96– 2.20	2.00– 2.29	1.95– 2.35	2.25– 2.84
Kentucky...................	2.05– 2.32	2.08– 2.18	2.02– 2.18	2.53	....
Illinois....................	2.05– 2.35	2.00– 2.29	1.99– 2.26	2.10– 2.45	2.06– 3.50
North Central group:					
Michigan and Wisconsin.....	1.95– 2.22	1.95– 2.22	1.90– 2.38	2.05– 2.40	2.25– 2.56
Southern group:					
North Carolina..............	2.29– 2.35	2.29– 2.47	2.18– 2.45	2.43– 2.47	2.61– 3.01
South Carolina..............	2.10– 2.50	2.30– 2.45	2.10– 2.40	2.33– 2.34	2.23
Georgia....................	2.08– 2.35	2.20– 2.40	2.10– 2.40	2.50	2.70
Florida....................	2.06– 2.38	2.25– 2.50	2.10– 2.37	....	....
Tennessee..................	2.20– 2.28	2.21– 2.36	2.20– 2.31	....	....
Alabama...................	2.21– 2.48	2.25– 2.35	2.27– 2.40	....	2.40– 2.60
Western group:					
Iowa......................	2.13– 2.22	2.10– 2.40	2.06– 2.30	2.17– 2.72	2.37– 2.66
Missouri...................	2.15– 2.26	2.10– 2.32	2.10– 2.30	2.30– 3.00	2.51– 2.62
Arkansas..................	2.35– 2.45	2.35	2.33– 2.38	2.45	2.70– 2.80
North Dakota...............	2.17– 2.37	....	2.06	....	....
South Dakota...............	2.21– 2.32	2.19– 2.26	2.21– 2.24	....	2.71
Nebraska..................	2.15– 2.52	2.10– 2.44	2.10– 2.42	....	2.54– 2.88
Kansas....................	2.28– 2.51	2.15– 2.54	2.14– 2.52	2.56	....
Oklahoma..................	2.45– 2.62	2.31– 2.74	2.29– 2.43	2.38– 2.49	2.66
Texas.....................	2.41– 2.82	2.22– 2.84	2.26– 2.74	2.50	2.67
Montana...................	2.65– 2.75	2.53– 2.75	2.53– 2.83	....	3.00– 3.13
New Mexico and Arizona....	2.03	2.85– 3.01	2.82– 3.17	....	....
Utah and Nevada...........	2.50– 2.85	2.75– 2.88	2.50– 2.85	....	....
Pacific coast group:					
Washington................	2.70	2.54– 2.70	2.45	2.54	....
California..................	2.84	2.50– 2.89	2.50– 2.90	....	2.70

On contracts for 100 tons to 999 tons, inclusive, of news-print paper there was little movement in the general level of prices between 1913 and 1915. There was a distinct increase during the first quarter of 1916, followed by a greater increase during the second quarter. In fact the minimum prices of the second quarter of 1916 were higher in most cases than the maximum prices of 1915. However, the number of contracts made during the first six months of 1916 was relatively small.

Comparing the range of prices in the second quarter of 1916 with the range in 1915, the most noticeable increases were as follows: In New York and New Jersey, grouped together, the range was from $1.98 to $2.35 in 1915, and from $2.09 to $3.27 in the second quarter of 1916; in Illinois the range was from $1.99 to $2.28 in 1915, and from $2.06 to $3.50 in the second quarter of 1916; in Pennsylvania, Delaware, and Maryland, grouped together, the range was from $1.98 to $2.30 in 1915, and from $2.08 to $3.16 in the second quarter of 1916; in North Carolina the range was from $2.18 to $2.45 in 1915, and from $2.61 to $3.01 in the second quarter of 1916; in Michigan and Wisconsin, grouped together, from $1.90 to $2.38 in 1915, and from $2.25 to $2.66 in the second quarter of 1916; in Ohio and Indiana, grouped together, from $2 to $2.29 in 1915, and from $2.25 to $2.84 in the second quarter of 1916; in Nebraska from $2.10 to $2.42 in 1915, and from $2.54 to $2.88 in the second quarter of 1916; in Massachusetts, Rhode Island, and Connecticut, grouped together, from $1.96 to $2.21 in 1915, and from $2.30 to $2.61 in the second quarter of 1916; in Montana from $2.53 to $2.83 in 1915, and from $3 to $3.13 in the second quarter of 1916; in Iowa from $2 to $2.30 in 1915, and from $2.37 to $2.66 in the second quarter of 1916; and in Missouri from $2.10 to $2.30 in 1915, and from $2.51 to $2.62 in the second quarter of 1916.

RANGE OF PRICES ON CONTRACTS FOR LESS THAN 100 TONS.—Contract prices for roll paper for less than 100 tons in carload lots ranged at a somewhat higher level than the prices on contracts involving larger tonnages.

During the period 1913 to 1915, inclusive, there was little change in the general level of prices on contracts covering such tonnage. On contracts made during the first quarter of 1916, however, there was some increase in prices. Very few contracts were made during the second quarter of 1916, but some of these were at considerable increases in price. As already stated, a number of small publishers whose contracts expired during this period could not secure new contracts, and were compelled to purchase their paper at market prices.

PRICES ON CONTRACTS COVERING DELIVERIES IN 1917.—During the second half of 1916 contract prices continued to advance. Contracts to cover the year 1917 were made by domestic and Canadian manufacturers at prices ranging from $2.50 to $3.50 per 100 pounds f. o. b. mill, most of the renewals being above $3. This represented an increase in the minimum of 65 cents and in the maximum of $1.50 per 100 pounds over the prices of 1915, which ranged from about $1.85 to about $2 at the mill.

In some cases contracts were made to cover deliveries in 1917 at $4.50 f. o. b. mill, an advance of from $2.50 to $2.65 per 100 pounds.

Low, HIGH, AND AVERAGE PRICES ON CONTRACTS FOR 100 TONS OR OVER.—In order to show whether the major part of the contract tonnage was sold at prices approximating the minimum or the maximum prices in the preceding tables a tabulation has been made showing for certain cities the lowest, highest, and weighted average prices of all contracts with publishers for 100 tons or more of newsprint paper in rolls during the period 1912–1916. This table is given below:

TABLE 11.—LOWEST, HIGHEST, AND AVERAGE PRICES ON CONTRACTS WITH PUBLISHERS FOR 100 TONS OR OVER OF NEWS-PRINT PAPER IN ROLLS, BY CITIES, 1912–1916 (FIRST HALF).

City.	Date of signing contract and price per 100 pounds, f. o. b. cars or sidewalk at destination.								
	1912			1913			1914		
	Lowest.	Highest.	Average.	Lowest.	Highest.	Average.	Lowest.	Highest.	Average.
Boston, Mass.[1]	$2.08	$2.30	$2.11	$2.05	$2.25	$2.08	$2.00	$2.20	$2.04
New York, N.Y.[1]	2.00	2.25	2.13	2.00	2.25	2.11	2.00	2.20	2.09
Philadelphia, Pa.[1]	2.05	2.25	2.15	2.03	2.25	2.08	2.07	2.18	2.13
Columbus, Ohio[3]	2.11	2.20	2.17	2.01	2.05	2.04	2.00	2.05	2.03
Chicago, Ill.[3]	2.09	2.25	2.20	2.05	2.25	2.13	2.03	2.15	2.13
Milwaukee, Wis.[3]	2.05	2.10	2.07	2.05	2.27	2.09	2.05	2.08	2.06
Kansas City, Mo.[3]	2.18	2.30	2.28	2.12	2.20	2.19	2.10	2.15	2.12
New Orleans, La.[3]	2.18	2.25	2.21	2.18	2.33	2.26	2.25	2.23	2.27

City.	Date of signing contract and price per 100 pounds, f. o. b. cars or sidewalk at destination—Continued.								
	1915			1916					
				January–March.			April–June.		
	Lowest.	Highest.	Average.	Lowest.	Highest.	Average.	Lowest.	Highest.	Average.
Boston, Mass.[1]	$2.02	$2.15	$2.08	$2.18	$2.18	$2.18	$2.25	$2.25	$2.25
New York, N.Y.[1]	2.00	2.20	2.09	2.00	2.15	2.11	....	....	....
Philadelphia, Pa.[1]	2.08	2.18	2.08	2.10	2.15	2.13	[3] 2.08	[3] 2.08	[3] 2.08
Columbus, Ohio[3]	2.00	2.01	2.00	2.04	2.04	2.04	2.40	2.40	2.40
Chicago, Ill.[3]	1.93	2.19	2.03	2.14	2.14	2.14	2.74	2.78	2.75
Milwaukee, Wis.[3]	1.95	2.10	1.99	2.08	2.08	2.08	2.30	2.30	2.30
Kansas City, Mo.[3]	2.10	2.13	2.11	....	....	....	2.49	2.51	2.50
New Orleans, La.[3]	2.21	2.25	2.22	2.40	2.40	2.40	2.58	2.58	2.58

[1] F. o. b. sidewalk at destination.
[2] Executed on May 9, 1910, but effective as of Jan. 1, 1916.
[3] F. o. b. cars at destination.

The table shows that in most years the average prices approximated more closely to the lowest prices than to the highest. This was especially true in 1915 and 1916. This results from the fact that contracts for a large tonnage are usually made at lower prices than those for a smaller tonnage.

There was a slight decrease in average prices in 1915 as compared with 1912 in all the cities shown, except New Orleans, where there was an increase of 1 cent per 100 pounds. The average prices in the first quarter of 1916 increased over the average prices in 1915 in all of the cities shown, the largest increase being 18 cents per 100 pounds in New Orleans. In the second quarter of 1916 the increase in the average prices over 1915 prices was much larger, except for Philadelphia. The largest increase was in Chicago, amounting to 72 cents per 100 pounds.

CONTRACTS IN FORCE SEPTEMBER 1, 1916.—The preceding tables show that prices on contracts made during the first quarter of 1916 advanced to some extent over prices on contracts made prior to January 1, 1916, and that contracts made during the second quarter of 1916 showed still further increases in price.

The number of contracts and the tonnage covered by those that were made during these periods for an annual supply of 100 tons and over and which were in force on September 1, 1916, are shown by Table 12 below. Contracts are shown separately for paper from mills in the eastern United States district, the Canadian district, and the north central United States district. The eastern United States district includes mills in New York and the New England States; the Canadian district includes mills in Quebec and Ontario; and the north central United States district includes mills in Michigan, Wisconsin, and Minnesota.

Contracts for paper from mills on the Pacific coast are not shown. It is sufficient for this district to state that nearly all of these contracts were made prior to September 1, 1915.

TABLE 12.—DATES OF SIGNING CONTRACTS WITH PUBLISHERS FOR 100 TONS OR OVER OF NEWS-PRINT PAPER, IN FORCE ON SEPT. 1, 1916.

Date of signing contract.	Eastern United States (339 contracts).[1]			Canada (86 contracts).[2]		
	Number of contracts.	Annual tonnage.	Per cent of tonnage.	Number of contracts.	Annual tonnage.	Per cent of tonnage.
Prior to Sept. 1, 1915	49	224,299	35.7	19	87,962	36.3
September–December, 1915	159	237,394	37.8	31	50,518	20.9
Total, prior to Jan. 1, 1916	208	461,693	73.5	50	138,480	57.2
January–March, 1916	58	104,162	16.6	15	50,190	20.8
Total, prior to Apr. 1, 1916	266	565,855	90.1	65	188,670	78.0
April–June, 1916	56	43,993	7.0	17	49,277	20.3
July–August, 1916	17	18,221	2.9	4	4,045	1.7
Grand total		628,069	100.0		241,992	100.0

[1] Includes mills in New York and the New England States.
[2] Includes mills in Quebec and Ontario with exception of the Fort Frances mill of the Minnesota & Ontario Power Co. in western Ontario.

TABLE 12.—DATES OF SIGNING CONTRACTS WITH PUBLISHERS FOR 100 TONS OR
OVER OF NEWS-PRINT PAPER, IN FORCE ON SEPT. 1, 1916—Continued.

Date of signing contract.	North central United States (75 contracts).[1]			Total (500 contracts).[2]		
	Number of contracts.	Annual tonnage.	Per cent of tonnage.	Number of contracts.	Annual tonnage.	Per cent of tonnage.
Prior to Sept. 1, 1915	24	33,885	35.4	84	346,144	35.9
September–December, 1915	10	24,070	25.2	209	311,982	32.3
Total, prior to Jan. 1, 1916	45	57,955	60.6	303	658,128	68.2
January–March, 1916	12	20,707	21.7	85	175,059	18.1
Total, prior to Apr. 1, 1916	57	78,662	82.3	388	833,187	86.3
April–June, 1916	15	16,025	16.8	88	109,295	11.3
July–August, 1916	3	840	.9	24	23,106	2.4
Grand total	....	95,527	100.0	....	965,588	100.0

[1] Includes mills in the States of Michigan, Wisconsin, and Minnesota, and the Fort Francis mill of the Minnesota & Ontario Power Co. in western Ontario.
[2] Covers mills in the United States and Canada, except those on the Pacific coast.

It will be seen that the greater part of the tonnage shown in each of the districts was under contracts made prior to January 1, 1916, when prices were low.

In the eastern United States district, 73.5 per cent of the total tonnage shown was under contracts made prior to January 1, 1916; 16.6 per cent under contracts made during the first quarter of 1916; and 7 per cent on contracts made during the second quarter of 1916. Corresponding figures for the Canadian district are 57.2 per cent, 20.8 per cent, and 20.3 per cent. For the north central district they are 60.6 per cent, 21.7 per cent, and 16.8 per cent.

The mills in the Canadian and the north central United States districts had under contracts made during the first six months of 1916 a larger proportion of their total tonnage shown than did the mills in the eastern United States district.

For the three districts combined, 68.2 per cent of the total tonnage shown was on contracts made prior to January 1, 1916; 18.1 per cent on contracts made during the first quarter of 1916; and 11.3 per cent on contracts made during the second quarter of 1916.

For the same three districts combined, contracts in force on September 1, 1916, covering 56.1 per cent of the total tonnage shown, expired prior to January 1, 1917, of which 49.5 per cent expired on December 31, 1916.

So large a proportion of low-priced contracts expiring during the fall of 1916 indicated that during 1917 renewed contract tonnage would have to bear a greater proportion of the increase in price, and that there would not be so great a disparity between prices on shipments of contract and current paper as occurred during the last half of 1916.

Section 4. Average receipts per 100 pounds at mill.

The changes that have occurred since January 1, 1913, in the average receipts per 100 pounds of manufacturers from the sale of news-print paper are shown by Table 13 below. The averages include all sales, both contract and market, and those to jobbers as well as those to publishers. They also include sales in Canada and other foreign countries.

The various mills included in the averages have been grouped according to location into five districts, designated in the table below as New England, New York, Canada, north central United States, and the Pacific coast. The north central United States district includes, in addition to the news-print mills in Wisconsin and Minnesota, a western Ontario mill. The Pacific coast district includes 1 mill in British Columbia in addition to those in the United States.

For the New York and the New England mills approximately 85 per cent of the news print produced during the period covered by the table was sold under annual contracts. The market fluctuations in the case of these mills as well as those of the Pacific coast where long-term contracts prevail are less quickly reflected in the trend of average receipts at the mill than in the case of the north central United States and the Canadian mills, which had a larger proportion of transient business, and also a larger proportion of tonnage under contracts renewed during the first half of 1916. The average receipts per 100 pounds at the mill were obtained by dividing the total receipts, less freight, drayage, and discounts, by the total tonnage shipped in each period.

TABLE 13.—AVERAGE RECEIPTS PER 100 POUNDS OF NEWS-PRINT PAPER AT MILL ON SHIPMENTS, BY DISTRICTS, 1913-1916 (FIRST HALF).

Period of shipment.	New England.			New York.			Canada.		
	Number of mills.	Shipped.	Average receipts per 100 pounds.	Number of mills.	Shipped.	Average receipts per 100 pounds.	Number of mills.	Shipped.	Average receipts per 100 pounds.
		Tons.			Tons.			Tons.	
1913	8	367,358	$1.91	12	339,500	$1.96	7	213,303	$1.86
1914	10	405,144	1.87	12	344,237	1.94	8	303,800	1.85
1915	10	410,165	1.88	12	322,116	1.92	9	336,472	1.82
1916 (first half)	10	220,944	1.89	12	175,444	1.98	9	193,344	1.85
January-June, 1916:									
January	10	35,639	1.87	12	27,077	1.94	9	30,154	1.81
February	10	34,160	1.89	12	25,503	1.94	9	32,768	1.82
March	10	36,838	1.89	12	31,988	1.96	9	33,896	1.84
April	10	38,110	1.90	12	29,512	1.97	9	33,805	1.86
May	10	38,364	1.91	12	29,706	2.01	8	31,367	1.88
June	10	37,833	1.91	12	31,678	2.05	8	31,444	1.92

TABLE 13.—AVERAGE RECEIPTS PER 100 POUNDS OF NEWS-PRINT PAPER AT MILL ON SHIPMENTS, BY DISTRICTS, 1913–1916 (FIRST HALF)—Continued.

Period of shipment.	North central United States.			Pacific coast.		
	Number of mills.	Shipped.	Average receipts per 100 pounds.	Number of mills.	Shipped.	Average receipts per 100 pounds.
		Tons.			*Tons.*	
1913...	6	130,986	$2.03	3	117,330	$2.20
1914...	7	160,807	1.97	3	125,561	2.17
1915...	8	187,262	1.95	3	131,318	2.13
1916 (first half)...............................	8	106,110	2.04	3	81,797	2.15
January-June, 1916:						
January.....................................	8	17,703	1.96	3	11,310	2.17
February....................................	8	17,102	1.93	3	11,890	2.04
March.......................................	8	18,463	1.98	3	12,863	2.19
April..	8	16,898	2.03	3	17,764	2.11
May...	8	18,380	2.08	3	13,656	2.21
June...	8	17,564	2.18	3	14,314	2.21

Comparing the average receipts per 100 pounds at mill in the different districts for the period 1913–1915, inclusive, it is seen that the lowest averages were received by the mills in the Canadian district, the range being from $1.82 to $1.86 per 100 pounds. Next in order came the New England district with a range from $1.87 to $1.91; then the New York district with a range from $1.92 to $1.96; then the north central United States district with a range from $1.95 to $2.03; and finally the Pacific coast district with the highest prices, from $2.13 to $2.20. All districts maintained the same rank during the first six months of 1916.

There was a slight decline in average receipts at mill in 1915 as compared with 1913 in all the districts. The greatest decrease was 8 cents per 100 pounds in the north central United States district, the receipts in 1913 being $2.03 while in 1915 they were $1.95. The smallest decrease was 3 cents per 100 pounds in the New England district, the receipts in 1913 being $1.91 while in 1915 they were $1.88. The receipts declined 4 cents per 100 pounds in both the New York and Canadian districts, and 7 cents per 100 pounds in the Pacific coast district.

The average receipts for the first six months of 1916 increased slightly over those in 1915 in all districts. The largest increase was 9 cents per 100 pounds in the north central United States district, the average increasing from $1.95 in 1915 to $2.04 in the first six months of 1916. The smallest increase was 1 cent per 100 pounds in the New England district, the receipts increasing from $1.88 in 1915 to $1.89 for the first six months of 1916. The increases in the other districts were 2 cents per 100 pounds in the Pacific coast district, 3 cents in Canada, and 6 cents in New York.

Taking the first half of 1916 by months, the greatest increase in average receipts per 100 pounds was in the north central United States district, where the average of $1.96 per 100 pounds in January increased to $2.18 in June, an increase of 22 cents per 100 pounds. The smallest increase during this period was in the New England district, where the average receipts increased from $1.87 in January to $1.91 in June, an increase of 4 cents per 100 pounds. The increase in both New York and Canada was 11 cents per 100 pounds.

The small increase in the average receipts of manufacturers during the first half of 1916, when prices were rising, is due to the fact that the great bulk of the tonnage was being delivered on contracts made before the rise in price began.

Section 5. Effect of contract system on prices.

Ordinarily a great increase in the price of any commodity is accompanied by a decrease in consumption. The increase in the price of paper during the first half of 1916, however, had only a slight effect on the total consumption, as nearly all the large publishers were protected by low-priced contracts, which in most cases still had six months or more to run and the increased price did not affect them. Moreover, the few who did sign new contracts at the higher prices were unable to reduce their consumption to any great extent, because in most cases their competitors, who were still getting paper at the old prices, were not disposed to curtail their consumption.

The fact that most of the contracts gave the publishers a leeway of from 5 to 10 per cent above or below the tonnage fixed as their ordinary requirements increased the tendency of the contract system to make consumption independent of price changes. Due to their increased need, most of the publishers demanded the maximum tonnage under their contracts. When this did not satisfy their requirements they went into the open market. This, of course, largely decreased the proportion of paper that would have been available for purchasers on current orders or on new contracts. The result was to make the prices to these latter purchasers very high, which in turn tended toward higher prices for contract renewals.

Section 6. Additional cost of paper to publishers in 1917.

The prices of contracts made at the close of 1916 generally ranged from $2.50 to $3.50 f. o. b. mill, the majority being $3 or above, which represented an advance to publishers of 65 cents in the minimum and of $1.50 in the maximum per 100 pounds. In some cases contracts were made in December, 1916, at $4.50 f. o. b. mill, an advance of from $2.50 to $2.65 per 100 pounds. What this advance in price will mean to publishers during the year 1917 is indicated by the following computation, which shows the increase in the cost of paper for certain newspapers using various tonnages. Freight and cartage charges were added to the 1917 prices to put them on the same basis as the 1916 prices.

Tonnage contracted for, 1917.	Increase in amount to be paid during 1917 as compared with that paid in 1916 for the same tonnage.	Tonnage contracted for, 1917.	Increase in amount to be paid during 1917 as compared with that paid in 1916 for the same tonnage.
135	$2,983	5,040	$166,320
240	4,800	6,000	143,460
600	13,800	6,000	313,560
900	21,780	7,200	164,160
1,200	27,360	8,500	193,800
2,000	46,800	30,000	674,400
5,000	114,000		

Information obtained by the Commission indicates that this increase in paper cost will generally exceed the annual profits of these publications and in some cases will be several times the profits made in any one year. If publications are considered which had contracts in 1915 but have been forced to buy in the open market since their contracts expired the increase in paper cost will be considerably larger in proportion to the tonnage used than for those newspapers shown above.

In addition to the greatly increased prices of contracts covering 1917, certain additional burdens and expenses must be borne by publishers as a result of changes made in the provisions of the contracts. (See p. 56.)

In attempting to meet the increased cost of news print the publishers have recourse to (1) cutting out unpaid subscriptions and returns from agents; (2) reducing the size of their paper by cutting out either news or advertising matter or both; (3) raising the price of subscriptions and street sales; or (4) raising the rates for advertising.

While these methods may be employed for a time without loss of revenue, if they are pursued beyond a certain point and for any length of time they may result in reduced receipts from sales and advertising.

Moreover, it is not possible in all cases to increase sales prices and advertising rates owing to competition from publishers who have unexpired contracts for paper at low prices, or have their own mills and who are thereby able to maintain low sales prices and advertising rates.

Section 7. Disparity in prices among publishers.

The rapid advance in the price of news print during 1916, coupled with the contract system, has resulted in a great disparity in prices paid by different publishers in the same locality for paper delivered during the latter part of the year. For example, publishers in the eastern and middle western groups of States who had contracts still in force that were made in 1915 were getting their paper in December, 1916, at about $2 to $2.20 f. o. b. destination, while publishers in the same localities whose contracts were renewed after September, 1916, were paying from $2.65 to $3.65 and in some cases even $4.65 f. o. b. destination for paper delivered the same month. Many publishers whose contracts had expired and could not be renewed were forced to go into the open market and to pay from $5.15 to $6.15 f. o. b. destination in carload lots for December deliveries.

The result has been that some of the publishers paying the higher prices have been put at a distinct disadvantage as compared with their competitors who were getting paper at the lower prices. Inasmuch as many of the old low-priced contracts run over well into 1917, this condition will continue for some time in certain localities.

In this connection a New Jersey publisher made the following statement:

> The matter of discrepancy in price is one that concerns the papers of the country even more than the large increase, because it puts one at a tremendous disadvantage with another. For instance, one paper in a town I heard of last night is paying $2.25 when a competitor is paying $6.

The publisher of a daily paper in one of the smaller cities in New York stated that he was paying $5 per 100 pounds for news print while his competitor was paying $2.66 on a contract that would not expire until April or May, 1917.

The disparity between the prices paid by country weeklies and city dailies is much greater at present than was the case in 1915. In 1915 the country weeklies were paying $3 or less per 100 pounds, while city dailies were renewing contracts at from $2 to $2.15 f. o. b. destination, a difference of 1 cent per pound or less. In December, 1916, however, the country weeklies were paying between $6.50 and $7.50 per 100 pounds, while most of the city dailies were renewing contracts at from $2.50 to $3.50, although in some cases renewals were made as high as $4.50 f. o. b. mill.

A representative of the smaller publishers made the following statement in December, 1916:

> * * * There never has occurred, with respect to the country papers, a condition so serious as that which now confronts them. They are facing a situation which, if continued, will mean ruin

to many men who have been conducting fairly prosperous business concerns.

*   *   *   *   *   *   *

It so happens that the alarming advance in the price of news print and other papers falls more heavily upon the country papers than those published in the cities, because they buy in smaller quantities and the advance in prices has been much greater to them than to those who buy in large lots and have contracts for large supplies.

*   *   *   *   *   *   *

Complaints are made by the country publishers of discrimination against them, a greater discrimination than is warranted by the fact that they purchase in smaller quantities, the differences between the prices paid by the country and city papers now being so much greater than two years ago. One publisher inquires why he should pay $7 per 100 for paper while daily papers in the larger cities are getting paper at $3.25 per 100.

The disparity in prices in the same localities is one of the difficulties confronting publishers in 1917. The big increase in the prices of contracts made for 1917 deliveries reduced somewhat the disparity between them and open-market prices, and the softening of the market which has occurred since January 1, 1917, has still further reduced this disparity. Among the publishers having contracts there also exists a considerable variation in prices. Some publishers have contracts which run through or partially through the year 1917 at $2 or less f. o. b. mill; others have contracts renewed around $2.50. A few are renewing at $4 or $4.50 per 100 pounds. This disparity in prices which will continue through 1917 adds to the serious consequences occasioned by the high cost of paper.

CHAPTER IV.

JOBBERS' COMMISSIONS AND MARGINS OF GROSS PROFIT.

Section 1. Introduction.

In this chapter are shown the gross profits obtained by the principal paper jobbers and selling agents on sales of news-print paper in 1916 and one or more prior years.

These gross profits are shown in the form of percentages on the cost price to the jobbers for merchandising or buy-and-sell transactions and in the form of rates of commission for commission business. In the former case, for example, paper costing $2 per 100 pounds and sold at $2.25 would show a margin of 25 cents or 12.5 per cent on the cost price. This margin of profit is gross, since it includes the cost of doing business.

Information relative to the distribution of news-print paper by jobbers and commission merchants was obtained from dealers in practically all the large commercial centers of the East, the Middle West, and the Pacific coast. In the Southern States the relatively small number of dealers handling news-print paper were not visited by representatives of the Commission owing to lack of time. The operations of these jobbers, as far as news print is concerned, are confined largely to the distribution of sheet news to publishers of weekly newspapers. The conditions under which news-print paper is bought and sold by jobbers in southern territory, it is believed, are not materially different from the conditions existing among the small jobbers in other sections, whose records were examined by the Commission.

There are two general methods of handling news-print paper by jobbers, namely, direct shipments from the mill, and shipments from the jobber's own stock. In the case of direct shipments the paper is shipped from the mill directly to the consumer according to instructions furnished by the jobber. In cases where the jobber has two or more customers in the same locality, their requirements in some instances are combined in one shipment and consigned to the jobber who delivers the paper from the railroad station to the consumer. In the case of sales from stock as distinguished from direct shipments, the paper is distributed by the jobber from his own warehouse as orders are received.

The margins of profit and commissions hereafter shown are only for transactions involving shipments directly from the mill to the consumer. Commission business is wholly of this character, as are also most of the buy-and-sell transactions for carload lots. In the latter case the purchase and sale of the paper by the jobber are practically contemporaneous transactions, each usually involving the same quantity of paper, so that his records show the purchase price and sales price for each transaction. Where orders are filled from stock carried in the jobber's warehouse or storeroom, the cost price is difficult of ascertainment. On this account no attempt has been made to secure the margins of profit on such sales.

It should be noted, also, that the margins are based on transactions in which the terms of delivery to the jobber and publisher were the same. For example, where the jobber purchased f. o. b. mill and sold f. o. b. destination or sidewalk, the transportation charges paid by the jobber were ascertained and included in his cost price before the margin of profit was computed.

There are a number of dealers in the more important commercial centers who buy and sell news print on a large scale, and in addition several concerns which dispose of the product of paper mills on commission. The news print handled by these commission houses is to a large extent obtained directly from the manufacturer and is sold, as a rule, in large quantities either to city dailies or to jobbers scattered throughout the country. These jobbers in turn supply daily papers of small circulation and country weeklies. Margins on sales by one jobber to another are not included in this discussion.

The jobbers from whom information was obtained have been arranged according to location into three groups as follows:

(1) *Eastern group.*—The Eastern group includes the New England States, the States of New York, New Jersey, Delaware, Maryland, and Pennsylvania. The figures presented for this territory are based on data obtained from an examination of the records of 27 dealers. In this group are included two important companies which sell the entire product of a number of paper mills on commission. Jobbing transactions in this territory include the distribution of a relatively large volume of news-print paper to the metropolitan dailies, at commissions ranging from 2.5 per cent to 5 per cent.

(2) *Western group.*—The Western group includes States extending from Ohio as far west as the Rocky Mountains. It includes the cities of Cincinnati, Detroit, Chicago, St. Louis, Kansas City, Omaha, St. Paul, and Minneapolis, which are distributing centers for news print produced by the paper mills of the Middle Western States bordering on the Great Lakes and western part of the Province of Ontario. The greater part of the requirements of weekly newspapers

in this section is supplied by jobbers. Information was obtained in this territory from 23 jobbers.

(3) *Pacific coast group.*—The Pacific coast group includes the States west of the Rocky Mountains. The newspapers of large circulation in this territory, to a great extent, buy paper directly from mills of the Pacific Northwest. An extensive jobbing business is carried on in the larger cities with publishers of dailies and weekly papers in smaller towns. The data presented for this territory are based on an examination of the records of seven jobbers.

The information obtained from the various jobbers has been so arranged as to show the margins on contract and open-market sales separately.

In order that the significance of the figures may be clearly understood, it is important to note that they represent, in some cases, only one of a series of cumulative margins included in the price paid by the publisher for paper. In the process of distribution to papers of relatively small circulation news print, in some instances, passes through the hands of two or more jobbers before reaching the publisher. The margins received by all jobbers in such cases are obviously materially greater in the aggregate than the last margin made on the final transfer of the paper to the consumer.

It must be remembered also that the margins are shown by the percentage they bear to the jobbers' cost prices. Therefore as prices advanced in 1916 the same percentage represented a larger actual profit, expressed in dollars and cents, than was the case in 1915. This is especially the case with market sales where the advance in price was greatest.

Section 2. Margins of profit on contracts.

The distribution of news-print paper by more important jobbers, as noted in the preceding chapter, is governed to a great extent by contracts executed contemporaneously with the manufacturer and publisher. Contract sales on commission are negotiated with publishers on the basis of terms previously agreed upon between the manufacturer and the commission merchant. In many cases, however, the jobber buys and sells on his own account, the difference in the prices paid and received constituting his margin of gross profit.

Most of the paper sold by jobbers on contracts is in rolls. For that reason the margins shown in this section are on roll paper only. Jobbers' commissions and margins on contracts for 18 tons or over of news-print paper in rolls are shown in the following table for the years 1913, 1914, and 1915, and for the first half of 1916:

TABLE 14.—JOBBERS' COMMISSIONS AND MARGINS, IN PERCENTAGES OF COST PRICE, ON CONTRACTS WITH PUBLISHERS FOR 18 TONS AND OVER OF NEWS PRINT PAPER IN ROLLS, 1913-1916 (FIRST HALF).

| Date of signing contract. | Commissions. | | | | Margins. | | | |
| | | Percent. | | | | Percent. | | |
	Tons.	Low-est.	High-est.	Aver-age.	Tons.	Low-est.	High-est.	Aver-age.
Eastern:								
1913...............................	70,473	1.4	5.0	3.7	14,356	0.1	9.6	4.0
1914...............................	106,771	2.4	5.0	3.3	20,853	1.6	13.7	4.3
1915...............................	97,405	1.5	5.0	3.1	19,349	.8	24.5	5.0
1916 (first half)..................	87,050	2.0	4.5	3.0	1,789	3.4	17.0	8.9
Western:								
1913...............................	4,375	1.3	3.0	1.9	36,289	.3	23.1	3.2
1914...............................	9,119	1.2	3.7	2.7	18,095	.8	15.6	4.2
1915...............................	80,163	1.0	4.0	1.3	28,814	.8	12.2	3.8
1916 (first half)..................	4,390	3.0	3.0	3.0	11,062	2.2	37.8	6.5

The relatively small tonnages for the first half of 1916 are due to the fact that few contracts are made during the first six months of the year.

The commissions of eastern jobbers ranged from 1.4 per cent to 5 per cent during the period covered. There was little change in the average commissions, the highest being 3.7 per cent in 1913 and the lowest being 3 per cent in the first half of 1916. The margins of profit on purchases and sales showed a wider range and a higher average than the commissions. The range was from 0.1 per cent to 24.5 per cent, the latter figure, however, being for 1915. There was a continuous advance in the average margin of profit from 4 per cent in 1913 to 8.9 per cent in the first half of 1916.

The commission business of western jobbers was done at rates ranging from 1 per cent to 4 per cent. The lowest average commission was 1.3 per cent in 1915 and the highest was 3 per cent during the first half of 1916. The margins on purchases and sales ranged from 0.3 per cent to 37.8 per cent, though it should be noted that the usual margins were a little below 12 per cent. The average margins increased from 3.2 per cent in 1913 to 6.5 per cent in the first half of 1916.

The average commissions of the eastern jobbers were slightly higher than those of the western jobbers except in the first half of 1916, when they were the same. Their average margins of profit on purchases and sales were also higher in all the periods.

As only a few contracts were made on the Pacific coast during the first half of 1916, no margins have been included in the table for jobbers in that group.

Section 3. Margins of profit on open-market sales.

In this section are shown jobbers' margins of profit on open-market transactions as distinguished from contract transactions. Most of this business is handled on a buy-and-sell basis.

MARGINS ON SHEET NEWS, 1915–1916.—The margins in percentages are shown in the following table by ranges for 1 to 17 tons, inclusive, of sheet paper, for the year 1915 and for the first and second quarters of 1916.

TABLE 15.—JOBBERS' MARGINS, IN PERCENTAGES OF PURCHASE PRICE, ON OPEN-MARKET SALES TO PUBLISHERS OF 1 TO 17 TONS, INCLUSIVE, OF NEWS-PRINT PAPER IN SHEETS, BY GROUPS, 1915–1916 (FIRST HALF).

Date.	Eastern.		Western.		Pacific coast.	
	Lowest.	Highest.	Lowest.	Highest.	Lowest.	Highest.
1915...	2.4	27.9	2.2	32.5	4.0	47.5
1916:						
First quarter........................	3.0	45.8	4.2	34.3	4.0	29.1
Second quarter.....................	8.3	55.6	4.3	¹ 101.0	7.6	32.5

¹ The weighted average margin of the jobber having this maximum margin was 41.9 per cent during the second quarter of 1916.

There was an increase in the minimum margins during the period covered by the table in all the groups shown. These minimum margins are more characteristic of the returns generally received by the jobbers than the maximum margins. The increase in the minimum margins for the eastern group was from 2.4 per cent in 1915 to 8.3 per cent in the second quarter of 1916. The increase in the Western group during the same period was from 2.2 per cent to 4.3 per cent. In the Pacific coast group the increase was from 4 per cent to 7.6 per cent.

The maximum margins increased during the same period in the Eastern and Western groups—in the former from 27.9 per cent to 55.6 per cent and in the latter from 32.5 per cent to 101 per cent. The weighted average margin of the jobber having the maximum margin of 101 per cent was 41.9 per cent during the second quarter of 1916.

The maximum margins in the Pacific coast group were 47.5 per cent in 1915 and 32.5 per cent in the second quarter of 1916.

PRICES AND MARGINS IN 1917.—In response to a request of the Commission a large number of jobbers furnished their cost and selling prices for news-print paper in rolls and in sheets during January and February, 1917. These prices have been tabulated for all transactions where shipments were made direct from the mill to publishers and where the purchase and sale were on the same basis, i. e., f. o. b. mill or f. o. b. destination. Sales on commission, however, are not included in the tabulations given below. The commission in most cases was 3 per cent.

The tabulation for roll news is as follows:

JOBBERS' PRICES AND MARGINS PER 100 POUNDS ON OPEN-MARKET SALES OF NEWS-PRINT PAPER IN ROLLS, JANUARY-FEBRUARY, 19:7.

[Direct Shipments.]

Quantity in pounds.	Jobbers' cost price f. o. b. mill.	Jobbers' selling price f. o. b. mill.	Margins.	
			Amount.	Per cent of cost price.
Carload:				
36,000	$3.50	$5.40	$1.90	54.3
41,705	4.00	4.75	.75	18.8
44,419	4.25	4.96	.71	16.6
54,286	4.75	5.50	.75	15.8
44,108	4.25	4.75	.50	11.8
51,080	4.25	4.71	.46	10.8
40,048	5.00	5.40	.40	8.0
38,211	5.39	5.75	.36	6.7
41,901	5.50	5.80	.30	5.5
41,082	5.00	5.25	.25	5.0
44,623	4.25	4.45	.20	4.7
47,113	5.50	5.75	.25	4.5
39,619	[1] 5.50	[1] 5.75	.25	4.5
47,197	4.25	4.44	.19	4.5
44,595	4.50	4.69	.19	4.2
40,820	5.00	5.15	.15	3.0
36,609	5.00	5.15	.15	3.0
Less than carload:				
5,800	[1] 5.00	[1] 6.00	1.00	20.0
1,600	[1] 5.09	[1] 6.00	.91	17.0
1,000	[1] 5.09	[1] 6.00	.91	17.9
7,400	[1] 5.09	[1] 6.00	.91	17.9
3,000	5.00	5.75	.75	15.0
7,600	[1] 5.00	[1] 5.75	.75	15.0
10,555	[1] 4.76	[1] 5.40	.64	13.4
2,840	5.00	5.50	.50	10.0
10,200	[1] 5.50	[1] 6.00	.50	9.1
10,472	[1] 5.51	[1] 6.00	.49	8.9
1,000	[1] 5.09	[1] 5.50	.41	8.1

[1] F. o. b. destination, or jobbers' shipping station.

On carload lots the highest margin was $1.90 per 100 pounds, or 54.3 per cent of the jobber's cost price. This unusually high margin was due largely to the low price—$3.50 per 100 pounds—that the jobber paid for the paper. On the other sales in carload lots the margins ranged from 15 cents to 75 cents per 100 pounds, or from 3 per cent to 18.8 per cent of the jobber's cost price. On less than carload sales the margins ranged from 41 cents to $1 per 100 pounds or from 8.1 per cent to 20 per cent of the jobber's cost price.

The tabulation for sheet news is as follows:

JOBBERS' PRICES AND MARGINS PER 100 POUNDS ON OPEN-MARKET SALES OF NEWS-
PRINT PAPER IN SHEETS, JANUARY-FEBRUARY, 1917.

[Direct Shipments.]

Quantity in pounds.	Jobbers' cost price f. o. b. mill.	Jobbers' selling price f. o. b. mill.	Margins.	
			Amount.	Per cent of cost price.
6,000	$4.00	$5.00	$1.00	25.0
12,000	4.00	5.00	1.00	25.0
2,000	4.85	6.00	1.15	23.7
1,000	4.85	6.00	1.15	23.7
2,569	5.75	7.00	1.25	21.7
2,040	6.00	7.25	1.25	20.8
2,410	6.00	7.00	1.00	16.7
2,000	5.55	6.35	.80	14.4
2,600	5.80	6.60	.80	13.8
8,000	4.75	5.40	.65	13.7
2,000	4.75	5.40	.65	13.7
6,000	4.75	5.40	.65	13.7
4,345	5.50	6.25	.75	13.6
2,048	6.00	6.75	.75	12.5
2,000	6.05	6.75	.70	11.6
2,190	5.75	6.40	.65	11.3
10,000	6.00	6.65	.65	10.8
3,290	6.50	7.10	.60	9.2
550	5.50	6.00	.50	9.1
4,073	5.75	6.25	.50	8.7
4,000	6.00	6.50	.50	8.3
2,000	6.00	6.50	.50	8.3
8,000	5.00	5.38	.38	7.6
10,000	6.30	6.75	.45	7.1
8,000	5.50	5.85	.35	6.4
1,972	5.30	5.60	.30	5.7
1,575	5.00	5.25	.25	5.0
11,160	5.60	5.85	.25	4.5

All the sales of sheet paper shown in the above tabulation are on less than carload lots. The margins range from 25 cents to $1.25 per 100 pounds, or from 4.5 per cent to 25 per cent of the jobbers' cost price.

It will be seen from the two preceding tabulations that, in general, the high prices charged by jobbers were due to the high prices they had to pay for the paper, although in some cases they made excessive margins on paper that they got at low prices.

Section 4. Jobbers' cost of doing business.

In response to inquiries as to the jobbers' cost of transacting business, representatives of the jobbers stated with reference to paper shipped directly from the mill to the consumer that sales in large quantities are profitable at a margin of 3 per cent. On direct shipments as a whole a margin of 5 per cent was declared by a representative of a middle western jobber to be sufficient to yield a fair profit to the dealer, while in the case of stock sales where the paper passes through the jobbers' warehouse a margin of from 15 per cent to 20 per cent was declared to be sufficient. With respect to all classes of transactions in news-print paper the jobbers' average cost of doing business was placed at from 12 per cent to 17 per cent of the cost price.

The principal items which enter into the jobbers' cost are said to be the cost of soliciting business, bookkeeping, bad debts, interest on the investment in warehouses, and cartage to and from the jobbers' warehouses. The jobbers' margins shown above obviously are not directly affected by the items of interest on investment in warehouses nor by cartage charges, these margins being based on transactions in paper shipped directly from the mill to the consumer.

Section 5. Conclusions.

A review of the foregoing data as to jobbers' margins in connection with the section on prices indicates that the operations of jobbers in news-print paper were as a whole more profitable in 1916 than during the period 1913–1915. That such is the case was in fact admitted by jobbers themselves at a public hearing of the Commission on conditions in the news-print industry. For sales on commission the rate of commission remained substantially the same, but the return to the jobber in 1916 exceeded the profits during the earlier period because of the advance in the price of paper on which the commission was based. On merchandising or buy-and-sell transactions in 1916 the price of paper and the jobbers' percentage of profit both advanced.

The return to the jobber at the higher margins and higher prices prevailing in 1916 has obviously involved the inclusion in the price to the publisher of a profit considerably in excess of the amount regarded as a fair return to the jobber. In the case of market transactions, for example, where prices to the publisher advanced from around $2.25 per 100 pounds in 1915 to as high as $6 and over in 1916, a jobber with a minimum margin of 5 per cent on his cost price of $2.14 in 1915 would receive less than 11 cents, whereas in 1916, with a minimum margin of 6 per cent on his cost price of $5.66, he would receive about 34 cents. The difference between jobbers' profits in 1915 and 1916 is, of course, much greater when considered on the basis of the maximum margins in each period.

It is thus apparent that the margins of jobbers were maintained or advanced as the price of paper advanced in 1916 to such an extent as to be a contributing cause to the greatly increased cost of paper to the consumer. This was particularly true in the case of publishers of papers of relatively small circulation who as a class are largely dependent on jobbers for their requirements and who to a great extent buy at the market prices. By January, 1917, however, the greatly increased cost of paper to publishers buying from jobbers was due mainly to the high prices charged by the mills.

It is pertinent in this connection to refer to the reasons advanced by jobbers in justification of the wide margin of profit shown in some cases. Customers with a poor credit rating or known to be slow pay, it is stated, are usually quoted higher prices than are quoted to those known to be prompt in making settlement. In other words, the credit risk is in the price. With the increase in price the risk becomes greater for the reason that there are many publishers who were able to pay promptly for a car of paper costing $800 in 1915, but who find it difficult to pay $2,000 for a similar quantity in 1916. The present high price of paper has caused the jobbers to resort more frequently to sight draft attached to bill of lading on shipments to customers considered poor pay. Most jobbers also claimed that the cost of replacement should govern the selling price regardless of the cost. If this theory is not followed, they say, the jobber is apt to find himself stocked with high-priced paper when the market declines. This contingency, however, as a general rule, would arise only in the case of sales from stock and not in the case of shipments directly from the mill to the consumer, which are the bases of the foregoing tabulations.

In addition to the effect of the higher margins of profit on prices, the jobbers handling news-print paper in 1916 were also responsible in part for the creation of a panic among publishers. Whether done with intent to profit thereby or not, the jobbers through their salesmen and by correspondence contributed to the exaggeration of the belief of an increasing shortage, which tended to cause prices to rise.[1]

---

[1] For copies of circulars sent out by jobbers in regard to high prices and scarcity of paper, see Exhibit 6.

CHAPTER V.

COSTS AND PROFITS OF MANUFACTURE.

Section 1. Introduction.

This chapter deals with the costs and profits of news-print paper manufacturers and contains information throwing light on the reasonableness of the prices presented in Chapter III. The cost and profit data were obtained direct from the books of manufacturers except for a few of the smaller companies, which furnished the figures by correspondence. The costs and profits of these smaller companies have not been included in the tables of averages shown in following sections, but are discussed separately.

Considerable difficulty was experienced in arriving at the true cost of manufacture, because of the great variation found in the methods of keeping costs. While some companies had very excellent systems, others had systems so incomplete that it was difficult to ascertain what their costs really were. This variation necessitated considerable readjustment and revision of the figures in order to put them on a uniform basis and make them in accord with the best accounting practice.

Even greater difficulty was experienced in arriving at the rate of profit on investment in the news-print industry, because the cost of investment could not have been obtained except by an exhaustive investigation requiring a much longer period of time than could be devoted to this matter. Several of the largest companies were amalgamations of smaller ones, the original cost of whose properties it was impossible to ascertain. In most cases it was found that the book investment of the news-print manufacturers was larger than information obtained from paper-mill engineers showed to be necessary to produce the particular tonnage, which indicated either that the plants have been written up or that the original costs were too high.

ITEMS ELIMINATED FROM COSTS.—In arriving at the true cost of manufacture, all intercompany and departmental profits have been eliminated. These arise in a number of ways. Some companies have wood-land subsidiaries or departments which transfer the pulp wood to the manufacturing company or department at a profit. One company, in particular, showed substantial profits on the operations of

82

its wood-land subsidiaries, while its news-print manufacturing business appeared to be run at a loss.

Some companies charge their ground wood and sulphite into news-print paper at a profit even when made at the same plant, this departmental profit being carried directly to profit and loss. Other companies charge these materials into news-print paper at cost when produced in the same mill, but charge them in at a profit when transferred from one mill to another.

All intercompany rentals have been eliminated from costs. These occur in a few cases where a plant is leased from a subsidiary or a rental is paid to a subsidiary for the use of water power. All forms of interest have been eliminated from costs, although but few companies included this item. Examples of such charges are bond interest, interest on borrowed money, bank discounts, interest on advances to subsidiaries, interest on timber-land investment, etc.

READJUSTMENT OF DEPRECIATION.—The great variation in the practice of companies with respect to depreciation made it necessary for the Commission to substitute computed depreciation figures for those found in the books of companies, in order that the costs should include a fair charge for this important item. Some companies did not charge any depreciation at all. Others charged off certain amounts each year according to temporary financial exigencies, carrying it directly to profit and loss. A few companies have had their properties appraised by engineers and have carried a depreciation item in their costs, based on expert information. The usual practice of news-print paper manufacturers is to charge all of the depreciation to news-print paper, or the final product. Only two companies distributed the depreciation charge back to ground wood and sulphite. Although this method is preferable, the Commission found it impracticable to make an accurate distribution, and hence in all cases has charged the depreciation entirely to news print. One or two companies have been charging off depreciation at such high rates that they have been reducing their plant investment more rapidly than is necessary. Other companies have charged their depreciation on an inflated book investment or have loaded present costs with depreciation which should have been charged in earlier years.

The Commission's depreciation figures were based on the testimony of expert mill engineers, which was to the effect that 3 per cent on the investment in plant and equipment is sufficient to depreciate the outlay in a modern mill. This conclusion was also reached by the Tariff Board in its report in 1911.[1] Assuming that the investment in depreciable property for a 100-ton mill is

---

[1] Pulp and News-Print Paper Industry; S. Doc. No. 31, 62d Cong., 1st sess., p. 74.

$1,800,000, the depreciation charge at 3 per cent would amount to about $1.75 per ton of product. This is based on a full production for 310 days in the year. The depreciation charges of several well-managed companies were found to approach quite closely to this figure.

In the cost tables shown in this report $1.75 a ton has been allowed on the cost of news-print paper for depreciation where the ground wood and sulphite were not purchased. Where the sulphite was purchased, $1.49 per ton was allowed; and where both the ground wood and sulphite were purchased, $1.05 was allowed. Such a scale of depreciation costs, while somewhat arbitrary, is believed to be fair, and if in error it is probably too high.

In this connection it should be pointed out that the output of a plant is not a satisfactory basis for computing depreciation and has only been adopted in this case because it was impossible to arrive at a more satisfactory basis.

MISCELLANEOUS READJUSTMENTS.—Variation in the practice of companies with respect to a number of items of expense has necessitated making some readjustments. Some of the more important ones are as follows:

Bad debts have been charged to selling expense and not included in factory costs.

Taxes, insurance, and administration—three items of general expense included in costs—have been distributed to news-print paper, sulphite, and ground wood instead of being charged entirely to news-print costs. The basis of distribution, where not made by the companies, was 50 per cent to paper and 25 per cent each to ground wood and sulphite. Where a company did not have a sulphite plant, the percentages used were 70 per cent to paper and 30 per cent to ground wood. These percentages were found to be in use by various companies.

Profits obtained from the sale of screenings, which are by-products in the production of sulphite and ground wood, were deducted from the cost of these materials, and profits obtained from the sale of waste materials such as felts, rubber, scrap iron, etc., were deducted from the item of repair materials in conversion costs. In a few cases where the information warranted the depletion charges found in the wood costs of companies obtaining pulp wood from lands owned in fee were reduced. In one case where it appeared that the company had failed to make a proper allowance, a liberal depletion charge was added to the costs.

The total changes made in the costs, as shown by the books of the companies, after debiting or crediting certain items found in the profit and loss accounts of companies, resulted in a deduction of only $1.48 per ton from the average cost for United States mills in 1915, and $1.15 per ton for the first half of 1916. For Canadian mills the revisions resulted in small additions to the cost as shown by the books.

Section 2. News-print paper costs, 1913–1916.

In order to ascertain what changes have occurred in the various items entering into the cost of making news-print paper since 1913, averages have been compiled for the principal mills in the United States and Canada for the years 1913, 1914, 1915, and the first six months of 1916. The figures included in these averages were obtained from mills representing more than 80 per cent of the total production in the United States for all years except 1913 and 90 per cent or more of the production for Canadian mills except for the first half of 1916, when the percentage was about 75.

The various items of cost are divided into three principal groups, (1) stock, which includes sulphite, ground wood, and other materials used; (2) conversion, which includes labor, power, fuel, and various supplies necessary to convert the raw materials into paper; and (3) general expenses, which include taxes, insurance, administration, etc. Depreciation, which is also a general expense, is shown separately. Selling expenses are shown in a later section dealing with profits.

Table 16 shows the average cost per ton, by years, of making news-print paper for United States mills, Canadian mills, and United States and Canadian mills combined for the period 1913 to June 30, 1916, inclusive.

TABLE 16.—AVERAGE COST OF MANUFACTURE PER TON OF NEWS-PRINT PAPER FOR UNITED STATES AND CANADIAN MILLS, 1913-1916 (FIRST HALF).

Item.	United States.				Canada.				United States and Canada combined.			
	1913	1914	1915	First half 1916	1913	1914	1915	First half 1916	1913	1914	1915	First half 1916
Number of mills	30	35	35	34	7	9	11	10	37	44	46	44
Tons produced	944,363	1,043,530	1,025,461	539,856	226,538	347,398	432,406	219,511	1,170,901	1,390,838	1,457,867	759,347
Stock:												
Sulphite	$8.02	$7.64	$7.47	$7.33	$7.97	$7.08	$7.01	$6.74	$8.01	$7.65	$7.33	$7.10
Ground wood	12.07	12.03	11.63	11.33	8.54	9.06	8.65	8.47	11.39	11.29	10.75	10.50
Fillers	.41	.38	.38	.22	.29	.34	.35	.30	.39	.37	.37	.25
Alum	.15	.15	.18	.17	.25	.23	.22	.23	.17	.17	.19	.19
Sizing	.11	.08	.10	.07	.16	.13	.07	.06	.12	.09	.09	.06
Miscellaneous	.59	.65	.73	.63	.47	.45	.63	.51	.56	.60	.70	.60
Total	21.35	20.63	20.49	19.75	17.68	17.89	16.93	16.34	20.64	20.17	19.43	18.70
Conversion:												
Labor	3.49	3.51	3.41	3.34	2.75	2.60	2.54	2.36	3.34	3.28	3.15	3.06
Felts	.80	.75	.68	.60	1.03	.96	.83	.95	.84	.80	.73	.77
Wires	.37	.35	.37	.43	.39	.34	.42	.40	.38	.35	.38	.42
Belting	.09	.11	.10	.10	.10	.09	.08	.07	.09	.11	.09	.09
Lubricants	.08	.08	.07	.06	.12	.10	.08	.07	.09	.08	.08	.07
Repairs	1.35	1.34	1.05	1.10	1.09	1.04	.94	.84	1.30	1.26	1.02	1.05
Fuel	2.04	2.03	1.97	2.25	2.35	2.13	1.96	2.18	2.10	2.05	1.97	2.23
Power and water rentals	.22	.27	.36	.33	.36	.36	.35	.33	.25	.29	.35	.33
Miscellaneous	.98	.98	.99	1.01	1.64	1.63	1.38	1.33	1.11	1.15	1.10	1.10
Total	9.42	9.42	9.00	9.40	9.83	9.25	8.58	8.53	9.50	9.37	8.87	9.15

General expenses:												
Taxes and insurance	.42	.50	.43	.50	.26	.26	.21	.19	.39	.44	.37	.41
Administrative	.54	.57	.60	.58	.86	.76	.66	.65	.60	.62	.62	.60
Total	.96	1.07	1.03	1.08	1.12	1.02	.87	.84	.99	1.06	.99	1.01
Cost, not including depreciation	31.73	31.42	30.52	30.23	28.63	28.16	26.38	25.71	31.13	30.60	29.29	28.92
Depreciation	1.69	1.66	1.69	1.70	1.69	1.72	1.73	1.72	1.69	1.68	1.70	1.71
Total cost	33.42	33.08	32.21	31.93	30.32	29.88	28.11	27.43	32.82	32.28	30.99	30.63

The table shows that the total cost of making news-print paper, including depreciation, was somewhat lower at the end of the three and one-half year period than at the beginning. The average cost for the United States mills covered by the table was $33.42 in 1913 as compared with $31.93 in the first half of 1916. Likewise, the average cost for the groups of Canadian mills shown in the table was $30.32 in 1913 as compared with $27.43 in the first half of 1916, a decline of $2.89 per ton. The average cost for United States and Canadian mills combined was $32.82 in 1913 and $30.99 in 1915 as compared with $30.63 in the first half of 1916.

The average cost for United States mills in the first half of 1916 exceeded that of Canadian mills by $4.50 per ton, $4.44 of which is due to the difference in the cost of sulphite and ground-wood pulp and conversion labor.

It should be noted in discussing these costs that the number of mills included in the average for each year is not exactly the same. This does not materially affect the results, however, because of the large tonnage included. If, for instance, the figures for 1915 and the first half of 1916 were made strictly comparable in this respect, the difference between them would be reduced somewhat but the cost for the 1916 period both for United States and Canadian mills would still be a few cents lower.

The average cost per ton for stock used by United States mills declined in the same manner as the total cost of making paper, but the conversion cost decreased between 1913 and 1915 and then increased in the first half of 1916 about 40 cents per ton. This increase was due mainly to an increase in the cost of fuel. General expenses increased in 1914, decreased in 1915, and increased again in the first half of 1916.

The average cost for stock used by the Canadian mills shown in the table was about 21 cents per ton higher in 1914 than in 1913 but declined in 1915 and the first half of 1916. The total conversion cost declined steadily from 1913 to the first half of 1916 being $1.30 per ton lower in the latter period. The total general expense showed the same downward trend.

Turning to particular items it is seen that the average cost of sulphite per ton of paper, on the whole, showed a slight decline in both the United States and Canada. The cost of ground wood per ton of paper also showed a small decline, except for Canadian mills, in 1914, where the inclusion of two new mills in the averages raised this cost to about 50 cents per ton. As sulphite and ground wood constitute about 60 per cent of the total cost of paper, the decline in the cost of these items was the most important factor causing the decline in the total cost of manufacture between 1913 and the first half of 1916. The items that showed the most noticeable increase in cost in the first half of 1916 were fuel, felts, wires, and repair materials. Higher prices, apparently, were paid for these materials on all new contracts. Of these various items the cost of fuel is the most important, since it represents about 6 or 7 per cent of the total cost of making paper.

While there was a general increase in the rate of wages in a number of mills during the spring of 1916, the cost of conversion labor per ton of paper did not increase, probably on account of the fact that increased production reduced the unit cost of this item. For example, the labor cost per ton of one large company declined steadily, although two increases in their scale of wages were made during the period covered. The output of this company, however, increased more than 45 per cent in three and one-half years.

AVERAGE COSTS FOR SECOND HALF OF 1916.—In December, 1916, the Commission secured cost data from 23 mills in the United States for a part of the second half of 1916. The period covered for most of these mills was four months; for a few it was three months, and for a few others it was five months. These mills during the first half of 1916 produced about 60 per cent of the total production of the United States and about 75 per cent of the tonnage included in the tables of the Commission for previous periods. No adjustments were made in these data, and the average results are compared with the unrevised costs as shown by the companies for the first half of 1916. Though seven mills showed a decline in costs for the latter period, the average cost for all mills was $1.50 per ton higher than the average cost for the same mills in the first half of 1916. This was due chiefly to the increase in the cost of ground wood, labor, and wires.

Although the cost of producing sulphite increased during this latter period, as shown in section 3 of this chapter, the cost of sulphite per ton of paper produced was less. Apparently this was due to the fact that the mills were using a smaller proportion of sulphite in the manufacture of news print.

In February, 1917, the Commission made a further examination of costs, obtaining data from 27 mills in the United States for either the month of December, 1916, or January, 1917. These mills represent about 65 per cent of the total production in 1916. The results for this one-month period show that the costs for the various mills had increased from $1 to $19.23 per ton, the average cost for all mills being $5.52 per ton higher than the average cost for the same mills in the first half of 1916.

PERCENTAGE OF COST.—The percentage of the total cost of manufacture of news-print paper attributable to each of the various items of cost for United States and Canadian mills combined during the period 1913 to 1916, first half, are shown by Table 17 following:

TABLE 17.—PERCENTAGE OF TOTAL COST OF PRODUCING NEWS-PRINT PAPER ATTRIBUTABLE TO PARTICULAR ITEMS—UNITED STATES AND CANADIAN MILLS COMBINED—1913-1916 (FIRST HALF).

Item.	1913	1914	1915	First half 1916.
	Per cent.	Per cent.	Per cent.	Per cent.
Stock:				
Sulphite	24.41	23.69	23.66	23.36
Ground wood	34.71	34.97	34.67	34.30
Fillers	1.18	1.14	1.20	.80
Alum	.52	.54	.63	.63
Sizing	.35	.30	.28	.21
Miscellaneous	1.72	1.15	2.26	1.96
Totla	62.89	62.49	62.70	61.26
Conversion:				
Labor	10.20	10.17	10.16	9.99
Felts	2.57	2.48	2.35	2.51
Wires	1.16	1.69	1.24	1.36
Belting	.25	.33	.30	.30
Lubricants	.26	.26	.25	.22
Repairs	3.97	3.91	3.29	3.54
Fuel	6.39	6.36	6.35	7.28
Power and water rentals	.76	.90	1.14	1.08
Miscellaneous	3.37	3.55	3.56	3.60
Total	28.96	29.04	28.64	29.88
General expense:				
Taxes and insurance	1.19	1.36	1.18	1.33
General and administrative	1.82	1.92	2.00	1.96
Total	3.01	3.28	3.18	3.29
Depreciation	5.14	5.19	5.48	5.57
Total cost	100.00	100.00	100.00	100.00

The table shows that during the three and one-half year period the cost of sulphite per ton of paper represented from 23.4 to 24.4 per cent of the total cost of manufacture and the cost of ground wood per ton of paper from 34.3 to 35 per cent of the total cost. The two items together represented from 57.7 to 59.1 per cent of the total cost of manufacture, while all other items of stock together represented only from 3 to 4 per cent. Of the total cost of ground wood and sulphite about 68 per cent is represented in the cost of pulp wood used, which item represents about 40 per cent of the total cost of making paper.

Total conversion costs per ton of news-print paper, of which about a third was labor, represented from 28.6 to 29.9 per cent of the total cost of manufacture. The other important conversion items were as follows: Fuel, 6.4 to 7.3 per cent; felts, wires, belting, and lubricants together, 4.1 to 4.4 per cent; repairs (including repair material and repair labor), 3.3 to 4 per cent; power, from 0.8 to 1.1 per cent; miscellaneous expenses (includes finishing, mill office, and other miscellaneous operating expenses), 3.4 to 3.6 per cent.

The total general expenses, excluding depreciation, per ton of news-print paper represented from 3 to 3.3 per cent of the total cost of manufacture, of which about one-third was attributable to taxes and insurance and two-thirds to other general and administrative expenses.

The item of depreciation, as computed by the Commission, represented from 5.1 to 5.6 per cent of the total cost of making news-print paper.

COST OF NEWS-PRINT PAPER, BY GROUPS OF MILLS.—The differences in the cost of production of the domestic news-print mills included in the table of average costs is shown by Table 18 below, which groups these mills into six classes and shows the number included, tonnage represented, percentage of the total tonnage, and the average cost for each group for the years 1913, 1914, 1915, and the first half of 1916.

TABLE 18.—COST OF PRODUCTION OF NEWS-PRINT PAPER IN UNITED STATES MILLS COVERED BY THE INVESTIGATION, ARRANGED BY GROUPS ACCORDING TO COST PER TON, 1913-1916 (FIRST HALF).

Group.	Number of mills.	Produced.	Per cent of total.	Average cost per ton.
1913.		*Tons.*		
I (less than $27).....................................	2	169,548	18.0	$26.51
II ($27 and less than $30).............................	3	82,773	8.7	27.57
III ($30 and less than $33)............................	1	75,290	8.0	30.97
IV ($33 and less than $36)............................	8	214,678	22.7	34.66
V ($36 and less than $40).............................	14	361,602	38.3	36.93
VI ($40 and over)....................................	2	40,472	4.3	49.80
Total..	30	944,363	100.0	33.42
1914.				
I (less than $27).....................................	3	192,705	18.5	26.27
II ($27 and less than $30).............................	1	59,681	5.7	27.17
III ($30 and less than $33)............................	4	210,113	20.1	31.66
IV ($33 and less than $36)............................	12	229,201	22.0	34.97
V ($36 and less than $40).............................	13	338,522	32.4	37.32
VI ($40 and over)....................................	2	13,308	1.3	40.43
Total..	35	1,043,530	100.0	33.03

TABLE 18.—COST OF PRODUCTION OF NEWS-PRINT PAPER IN UNITED STATES MILLS COVERED BY THE INVESTIGATION, ARRANGED BY GROUPS ACCORDING TO COST PER TON, 1913–1916 (FIRST HALF)—Continued.

Group.	Number of mills.	Produced.	Per cent of total.	Average cost per ton.
1915.		*Tons.*		
I (less than $27).................................	3	195,830	19.1	$26.64
II ($27 and less than $30).........................	2	138,934	13.5	28.51
III ($30 and less than $33).........................	8	260,505	25.4	31.64
IV ($33 and less than $36).........................	11	276,672	27.0	34.75
V ($36 and less than $40).........................	8	120,199	11.7	37.74
VI ($40 and over).................................	3	33,321	3.3	43.67
Total..	35	1,025,401	100.0	32.21
1916 (first half).				
I (less than $27).................................	2	47,436	8.8	25.56
II ($27 and less than $30).........................	4	146,850	27.2	28.10
III ($30 and less than $33).........................	10	150,233	27.8	31.30
IV ($33 and less than $36).........................	8	117,729	21.8	34.96
V ($36 and less than $40).........................	6	34,441	6.4	37.03
VI ($40 and over).................................	4	43,147	8.0	41.76
Total..	34	539,836	100.0	31.93

In 1913, while the average cost of all the 30 mills was $33.42 per ton, the cost of the groups ranged from $26.51 for the two lowest mills combined to $40.80 for the two highest mills combined. The range for individual mills was from $26.38 to $40.90 per ton. About 27 per cent of the total tonnage was produced for less than $30 per ton, and 57.4 per cent was produced for less than $36 per ton.

The range of costs for the 35 mills by groups in 1914 was from $26.27 for the three lowest mills combined to $40.43 for the two highest mills combined, while the average cost for 35 mills was $33.08. The lowest individual mill cost was $26.14 per ton, and the highest $40.47. In this year only 24.2 per cent of the total tonnage was produced for less than $30 per ton, and 66.3 per cent was produced for less than $36 per ton.

In 1915 the costs for 35 mills by groups ranged from $26.64 per ton for the three lowest mills combined to $43.67 for the three highest mills combined, while the average cost for 35 mills was $32.21. The lowest cost for a single mill was $25.77 per ton, and the highest $44.41 per ton. In this year about 33 per cent of the total tonnage was produced for less than $30 per ton, and 85 per cent for less than $36 per ton.

In the first half of 1916 the range of costs for 34 mills by groups was from $25.56 per ton for the two lowest mills combined to $41.76 per ton for the four highest mills combined, the average cost for 34 mills being $31.93 per ton. The lowest cost in this period was $24.93 per ton and the highest cost $46.94 per ton. In this period 36 per cent of the total tonnage was produced for less than $30 per ton, and 85.6 per cent for less than $36 per ton. Sixteen mills had an average cost of less than $33 per ton as compared with only 13 mills in 1915.

It should be noted that the proportion of news-print paper produced by mills having a cost of $40 or over increased during the three and one-half years from 4.3 per cent to 8 per cent of the tonnage covered by the table. Also the range in costs of individual mills was greater for the first half of 1916 than for 1915, the high cost in the 1916 period, $46.94 per ton, being considerably higher. (See p. 95.)

In 1913, of the 7 Canadian mills whose costs were obtained, 3 would fall in Group II, 3 in Group III, and 1, with a cost of $37.17, in Group V. In 1914, 4 Canadian mills would fall in Group II and 5 in Group III, there being none that would fall in either of the remaining groups. In 1915, 3 of the 11 Canadian mills would fall in Group I, the lowest cost being $25.71 per ton, 5 would fall in Group II, and 3 in Group III. In the first half of 1916, 4 of the 10 Canadian mills would fall in Group I, with a cost less than $27 per ton, 4 would fall in Group II, and 2 in Group III. The lowest cost for any Canadian mill in this year was $25.68 per ton.

Incomplete cost data were secured, largely by correspondence, from 15 additional mills in the United States, which data have not been included in the tables above. These mills produced in 1915 and the first half of 1916 about 13 per cent of the total production. The average cost for these mills as reported to the Commission, and without any revision, was $37.97 per ton in 1915 and $37.81 for the first half of 1916. Had these additional mills been included in Table 16 above, more than 95 per cent of the domestic production would have been accounted for in 1915 and about 93 per cent in the first half of 1916. The average cost for the United States with these additional mills included would have been $32.96 per ton in 1915 and $32.73 per ton in the first half of 1916.

If the 15 additional mills had been included in Table 18, 1 would fall in Group III, 4 in Group IV, 5 in Group V, and 5 in Group VI in 1915, and in the first half of 1916, 1 would fall in Group III, 4 in Group IV, 4 in Group V, and 5 in Group VI, while 1 mill did not manufacture news print in this year.

COST OF NEWS-PRINT PAPER BY INDIVIDUAL MILLS.—The differences in the principal items of cost of production of news-print paper for the domestic mills are shown in Table 19 below, which gives separately for each mill, whose cost was secured from its books, the cost of sulphite, ground wood, miscellaneous stock materials, conversion, general expenses, and depreciation per ton of news-print paper produced for the year 1915 and the first half of 1916. The mills are arranged in order of the lowest costs. Hence a particular mill may not have the same number in 1915 as in 1916.

Table 13.—COST OF MANUFACTURE PER TON OF NEWS-PRINT PAPER FOR PRINCIPAL UNITED STATES MILLS, 1915-1916 (FIRST HALF).

Mill No.	Stock.				Total conver-sion.	General expenses.	Deprecia-tion.	Total cost.
	Sulphite.	Ground wood.	Miscella-neous.	Total.				
1915:								
1.................	$7.23	$9.00	$1.62	$17.85	$5.06	$1.11	$1.75	$25.77
2.................	6.52	8.96	.67	16.09	8.46	.38	1.75	26.68
3.................	8.18	8.73	1.65	18.56	6.55	1.08	1.75	26.94
4.................	6.90	8.59	.68	16.17	9.21	.39	1.75	27.52
5.................	6.36	10.85	1.80	19.01	7.78	.77	1.74	29.30
6.................	7.48	10.26	1.25	18.99	7.77	1.97	1.72	30.45
7.................	7.20	11.17	1.42	19.79	8.42	.90	1.48	30.59
8.................	5.39	12.78	1.52	19.69	8.43	1.20	1.49	30.81
9.................	6.69	12.46	1.43	20.58	7.41	1.55	1.48	31.02
10.................	9.22	12.35	1.59	23.16	6.27	1.17	1.45	32.05
11.................	7.02	10.70	.31	18.03	10.95	1.38	1.75	32.11
12.................	6.82	11.45	1.61	19.38	9.95	.64	1.75	32.22
13.................	7.08	12.33	.74	20.15	10.24	.51	1.75	32.65
14.................	4.91	11.56	1.40	17.87	12.25	1.34	1.75	33.21
15.................	5.91	11.43	1.59	18.96	11.51	1.23	1.75	33.45
16.................	7.03	14.37	2.08	23.48	8.16	.60	1.66	33.90
17.................	6.10	14.03	1.65	21.78	10.12	.87	1.71	34.48
18.................	8.55	12.70	.77	22.02	8.99	1.82	1.75	34.58
19.................	8.16	12.68	2.28	23.12	8.63	1.41	1.64	35.10
20.................	6.06	13.07	2.04	21.17	11.15	1.09	1.74	35.15
21.................	8.40	10.53	.82	19.75	11.77	1.90	1.75	35.17
22.................	6.93	16.03	2.01	24.97	8.01	.69	1.53	35.20
23.................	6.72	15.41	1.58	23.71	8.85	1.04	1.69	35.29
24.................	6.80	13.18	1.80	21.78	11.34	.99	1.74	35.85
25.................	10.64	11.78	2.69	24.51	8.77	1.37	1.41	36.06
26.................	6.61	14.87	1.70	23.18	10.73	1.12	1.75	36.78
27.................	9.13	14.09	3.07	26.29	8.22	.99	1.49	36.99
28.................	8.59	14.03	.83	23.45	10.81	1.34	1.40	37.00
29.................	9.44	11.70	1.57	22.71	11.05	1.97	1.37	37.10
30.................	8.52	13.79	.90	23.21	10.64	1.64	1.75	37.24
31.................	7.79	12.75	1.58	22.12	11.38	2.72	1.46	37.68
32.................	12.44	12.78	1.63	26.85	8.85	1.80	1.64	39.14
33.................	4.55	16.03	2.43	23.61	13.35	1.84	1.75	40.55
34.................	8.44	14.43	2.19	25.06	14.37	1.57	1.75	42.75
35.................	10.69	13.73	.90	25.32	16.18	1.16	1.75	44.41
Average......	7.47	11.03	1.39	20.49	9.00	1.03	1.69	32.21

TABLE 15.—COST OF MANUFACTURE PER TON OF NEWS-PRINT PAPER FOR PRINCIPAL UNITED STATES MILLS, 1915-1916 (FIRST HALF)—Continued.

Mill No.	Stock.				Total conversion.	General expenses.	Depreciation.	Total cost.
	Sulphite.	Ground wood.	Miscellaneous.	Total.				
1916 (first half):								
1	$7.70	$8.18	$1.21	$17.09	$5.36	$.73	$1.75	$34.93
2	7.41	8.71	1.27	17.39	5.96	.71	1.75	25.81
3	6.70	9.08	.04	15.82	9.31	.50	1.75	27.38
4	7.51	8.39	.91	16.81	9.13	.52	1.75	28.21
5	6.13	11.35	1.51	18.99	6.30	1.90	1.49	28.68
6	6.48	10.67	1.07	18.22	8.17	.82	1.74	28.95
7	4.32	13.87	.74	18.93	7.63	2.63	1.45	30.34
8	7.12	8.80	.22	16.14	10.73	1.75	1.75	30.37
9	5.82	13.44	1.65	20.91	7.43	1.27	1.48	31.09
10	6.95	9.81	1.71	18.47	9.09	2.02	1.75	31.33
11	5.87	11.79	.90	18.56	10.39	.71	1.75	31.41
12	8.12	11.06	.40	19.52	8.39	1.78	1.75	31.44
13	7.01	11.30	.40	18.71	11.28	.74	1.75	32.48
14	4.80	12.21	1.10	18.11	11.63	1.12	1.75	32.61
15	6.71	10.43	1.15	18.29	11.65	1.15	1.75	32.84
16	6.61	11.71	1.65	19.97	9.69	1.58	1.75	32.99
17	7.72	13.06	1.06	21.84	8.93	.79	1.46	33.02
18	6.96	14.02	1.42	22.40	8.63	.68	1.70	33.41
19	6.02	13.74	1.08	20.84	11.14	.92	1.75	34.65
20	9.49	11.83	2.61	23.93	8.98	1.28	1.34	35.53
21	8.02	14.16	1.11	23.29	9.61	1.08	1.75	35.73
22	7.97	10.92	.73	19.62	12.66	1.73	1.75	35.76
23	6.65	16.55	1.13	24.33	9.04	.85	1.56	35.78
24	7.93	13.01	.51	21.45	10.75	1.84	1.75	35.79
25	8.34	12.73	1.33	22.40	11.28	.98	1.75	36.43
26	8.61	11.69	2.30	22.60	10.68	1.99	1.39	36.66
27	8.35	13.37	.76	22.48	11.53	1.29	1.38	36.68
28	9.52	12.89	3.62	26.03	8.17	1.41	1.49	37.10
29	7.67	12.76	1.85	22.28	12.84	1.66	1.75	37.93
30	7.39	14.66	1.38	23.43	12.22	1.15	1.75	38.55
31	7.01	13.68	3.10	23.82	12.73	2.00	1.48	40.03
32	13.07	11.89	2.55	27.51	9.68	1.75	1.69	40.63
33	8.75	15.22	1.22	25.19	15.76	1.32	1.75	44.02
34	11.32	16.59	1.68	29.59	14.46	1.14	1.75	46.94
Average	7.33	11.33	1.09	19.75	9.40	1.08	1.70	31.93

The table brings out the remarkably wide range of mill costs for all items except depreciation which was computed by the Commission, as stated above. (See p. 83.)

In 1915 the cost of sulphite ranged from $4.55 per ton in mill No. 33 to $12.44 in mill No. 32, while in the first half of 1916 the range was from $4.32 in mill No. 7 to $13.07 per ton of paper produced in mill No. 32. The cost of ground wood in 1915 ranged from $8.59 for mill No. 4 to $16.63 per ton of paper for mill No. 33, while in the first half of 1916 the range was from $8.18 for mill No. 1 to $16.59 for mill No. 34. The cost of miscellaneous stock materials also differed widely in the various mills due, no doubt, to some extent to the difference in the quantities of clay, alum, sizing, etc., used. The total stock cost in 1915 ranged from $16.09 per ton in mill No. 2 to $26.85 in mill No. 32, and in the first half of 1916 from $15.82 per ton in mill No. 3 to $29.59 in mill No. 34. Mills having the lowest total cost generally have the lowest stock cost, since the cost of stock materials constitutes such a large proportion of the total cost of manufacture. Of the 19 mills in the first half of 1916 whose total costs were less than $35 per ton, in only 4 mills did the stock cost exceed $20 per ton, and of the 15 mills whose total cost exceeded $35 per ton, in only 1 was the stock cost less than $20 per ton.

The conversion costs in the various mills show as wide a range as stock costs. In 1915 the range was from $5.06 per ton for mill No. 1 to $16.18 for mill No. 35, while in the first half of 1916 the range was from $5.36 per ton for mill No. 1 to $15.76 for mill No. 33. In the first half of 1916 of the 16 mills, whose conversion costs exceeded $10 per ton, the total cost was less than $35 per ton in only 6 mills. Conversion costs are affected by various factors, such as location of mills with respect to fuel and power, efficiency of equipment, difference in wages paid, etc.

General expenses ranged in 1915 from $0.38 per ton for mill No. 2 to $2.72 per ton for mill No. 31, and in the first half of 1916 from $0.50 per ton for mill No. 3 to $2.03 per ton for mill No. 7. In the first half of 1916 of the 20 mills, whose average cost for general expenses exceeded $1.10 per ton, the total cost was less than $35 per ton in 9 mills. General expenses are affected mainly by differences in officers' salaries and other administrative expenses.

Depreciation ranged from less than $1.35 per ton of product in mills which produce no sulphite and only a portion of the ground wood used to $1.75 per ton in mills which produce all of both materials used.

Section 3. Sulphite costs, 1913–1916.

The changes that have taken place in the cost of producing sulphite in United States and Canadian mills during the years 1913, 1914, 1915, and the first half of 1916 are shown in Table 20 below. These averages include all of the mills having sulphite plants from which news-print costs were obtained and show the details of the item "sulphite" in the news-print costs shown in Table 16. Nine of the news-print mills in the United States did not have sulphite plants, but they produced only about 10 per cent of the total tonnage of news print manufactured. All of the Canadian mills included in the table of news-print costs had their own sulphite plants.

No depreciation is shown, the charge being included in the news-print paper costs as explained above. (See p. 83.)

TABLE 20.—AVERAGE COST OF MANUFACTURE PER TON OF SULPHITE FOR UNITED STATES AND CANADIAN MILLS, 1913-1916 (FIRST HALF).

Item.	United States.				Canada.				United States and Canada combined.			
	1913	1914	1915	First-half 1916.	1913	1914	1915	First half 1916.	1913	1914	1915	First half 1916.
Number of mills	19	21	22	20	5	7	9	8	24	28	31	28
Tons produced	305,531	321,533	326,093	195,647	63,349	111,930	142,959	77,219	368,880	423,463	469,052	272,866
Stock:												
Sulphur	$3.14	$3.13	$2.97	$2.70	$3.33	$3.09	$3.04	$2.97	$3.18	$3.12	$3.00	$2.84
Lime and limestone	.90	.83	.84	.82	.39	.39	.45	.38	.81	.75	.72	.70
Wood	17.27	16.84	17.16	17.42	14.27	15.07	14.32	13.82	16.76	16.38	16.29	16.40
Total	21.31	20.85	20.97	21.03	18.04	18.55	17.81	17.17	20.75	20.26	20.01	19.94
Conversion:												
Labor	3.67	3.76	3.51	3.39	2.49	2.49	2.44	2.00	3.47	3.43	3.18	3.00
Felts	.10	.10	.09	.11	.09	.09	.11	.13	.10	.10	.10	.12
Wires	.02	.02	.02	.03	.01	.01	.01	.02	.02	.02	.02	.03
Belting	.13	.13	.09	.12	.07	.05	.04	.04	.12	.11	.08	.09
Lubricants	.03	.03	.03	.03	.02	.02	.02	.01	.03	.03	.03	.02
Repairs	1.79	1.75	1.68	1.80	1.41	1.32	1.12	.94	1.72	1.64	1.51	1.56
Fuel	2.36	2.14	2.08	2.28	3.25	2.97	2.33	2.22	2.51	2.35	2.15	2.26
Power and water rentals	.35	.63	.50	.53	.50	.66	.59	.63	.38	.63	.53	.55
Miscellaneous	.49	.48	.52	.52	.92	.68	.79	.75	.56	.54	.60	.59
Total	8.94	9.04	8.61	8.81	8.76	8.29	7.44	6.74	8.91	8.85	8.25	8.22
General expenses:												
Taxes and insurance	.41	.45	.43	.43	.25	.21	.21	.21	.38	.39	.36	.37
Administrative	.54	.71	.69	.51	.88	.64	.75	.73	.60	.69	.71	.57
Total	95	1.10	1.12	.94	1.13	.85	.96	.94	.98	1.08	1.07	.94
Total cost[1]	31.20	31.05	30.70	30.78	27.93	27.69	26.21	24.85	30.64	30.19	29.33	29.10

[1] Exclusive of depreciation which on the average would be about $1.17 per ton of sulphite.

The table shows little variation in the average cost of producing sulphite in the United States and Canada combined during the period from 1913 to the middle of 1916. The average cost for the varying number of mills in the United States and Canada was $30.64 per ton in 1913, $30.19 in 1914, $29.33 in 1915, and $29.10 in the first half of 1916. If the figures were put upon a more strictly comparable basis, by using the same mills for each year, the averages for 1915 and the first half of 1916 would not be materially changed.

AVERAGE COSTS FOR SECOND HALF OF 1916.—In December, 1916, the Commission secured additional cost data covering a part of the year since July 1, 1916, from 16 mills making sulphite in the United States. While these costs covered periods ranging from three to five months, the average period covered was about four months. These mills during the first half of 1916 produced 79 per cent of the total tonnage included in Table 20 above. No adjustments have been made in these figures, and the average results are compared with the costs as shown on the books of the companies for the first half of 1916. The average cost of sulphite for the above 16 mills during the latter part of the year was $1.75 per ton higher. This was due chiefly to the increase in the cost of wood, sulphur, labor, and repairs. Companies buying pulp wood were paying materially higher prices during the latter part of 1916.

In February, 1917, cost data were secured from 15 mills in the United States for the month of December, 1916, or January, 1917. These mills during the first half of 1916 produced 74 per cent of the total tonnage included. The average cost of sulphite for these mills in this period was $3.38 per ton higher than the unrevised cost for the same mills during the first half of 1916.

PERCENTAGE OF COST.—The percentage of the total cost of producing sulphite attributable to particular items is shown by Table 21 following for United States and Canadian mills combined for the years 1913, 1914, 1915, and the first half of 1916.

TABLE 21.—PERCENTAGE OF TOTAL COST OF PRODUCING SULPHITE ATTRIBUTABLE TO PARTICULAR ITEMS—UNITED STATES AND CANADIAN MILLS COMBINED—1913-1916 (FIRST HALF).

Item.	1913	1914	1915	First half 1916.
	Per cent	Per cent.	Per cent.	Per cent.
Stock:				
Sulphur	10.38	10.35	10.21	9.77
Lime and limestone	2.65	2.49	2.46	2.39
Wood	54.69	54.28	55.53	56.36
Total	67.72	67.12	68.20	68.52
Conversion:				
Labor	11.32	11.38	10.85	10.30
Felts	.31	.32	.34	.40
Wires	.07	.05	.06	.10
Belting	.39	.36	.26	.32
Lubricants	.09	.09	.09	.08
Repairs	5.61	5.43	5.15	5.36
Fuel	8.20	7.80	7.33	7.77
Power and water rentals	1.24	2.09	2.00	1.91
Miscellaneous	1.84	1.77	2.06	2.01
Total	29.07	29.30	28.14	28.25
General expense:				
Taxes and insurance	1.25	1.28	1.24	1.26
General and administrative	1.96	2.30	2.42	1.97
Total	3.21	3.58	3.66	3.23
Total cost [1]	100.00	100.00	100.00	100.00

[1] Exclusive of depreciation.

The cost of stock in producing sulphite represents about 67.5 per cent of the total cost, of which pulp wood, the principal material used, represents about 55 per cent and sulphur and limestone represent about 12.5 per cent.

The conversion cost represents from 28 to 29 per cent of the total cost of producing sulphite. The principal items of conversion cost are labor, which represents from about 10 to 11 per cent of the total cost, and fuel, which represents from about 7 to 8 per cent of the total cost.

COST OF PRODUCTION OF SULPHITE, BY GROUPS OF MILLS.—The differences in the costs of domestic sulphite mills are shown by Table 22 below, which groups the mills according to the cost per ton and shows the number included, the tonnage represented, the percentage of the total production, and the average cost for each group for the years 1913, 1914, 1915, and first half of 1916.

TABLE 22.—COST OF PRODUCTION OF SULPHITE IN UNITED STATES MILLS COVERED BY THE INVESTIGATION, ARRANGED BY GROUPS ACCORDING TO COST PER TON, 1913-1916 (FIRST HALF).

Group.	Number of mills.	Pro- duced.	Per cent of total.	Average cost per ton.[1]
1913.		*Tons.*		
I (less than $27)	2	55,986	18.3	$24.84
II ($27 and less than $30)...............................	2	29,575	9.7	27.52
III ($30 and less than $33).............................	6	104,062	34.1	31.62
IV ($33 and less than $36).............................	6	91,423	29.9	34.08
V ($36 and over).......................................	3	24,485	8.0	37.65
Total..	19	305,531	100.0	31.20
1914.				
I (less than $27)......................................	2	60,311	18.6	25.03
II ($27 and less than $30).............................	2	28,597	8.9	27.48
III ($30 and less than $33)............................	9	143,064	44.5	31.51
IV ($33 and less than $36)............................	6	73,263	22.8	35.36
V ($36 and over)......................................	2	16,298	5.2	36.34
Total..	21	321,533	100.0	31.05
1915.				
I (less than $27)......................................	3	82,311	25.2	24.67
II ($27 and less than $30).............................	4	58,049	17.8	28.17
III ($30 and less than $33)............................	4	65,825	20.2	31.34
IV ($33 and less than $36)............................	6	85,658	26.6	34.79
V ($36 and over)......................................	5	33,250	10.2	38.14
Total..	22	326,093	100.0	30.70
1916 (first half).				
I (less than $27)......................................	3	28,125	14.4	22.97
II ($27 and less than $30).............................	3	42,305	21.6	27.63
III ($30 and less than $33)............................	4	49,571	25.3	31.09
IV ($33 and less than $36)............................	6	43,617	22.3	34.06
V ($36 and over)......................................	4	32,029	16.4	36.85
Total..	20	195,647	100.0	30.7

[1] Exclusive of depreciation.

While the figures for the different years are not strictly comparable on account of the different number of mills for which data were available, they show that the percentage of sulphite produced by mills having a cost less than $33 per ton was fairly uniform, being 62 per cent in 1913 and 61 per cent in the first half of 1916. The proportion of sulphite produced by the groups having a cost of $36 or over, however, increased from 8 per cent in 1913 to over 16 per cent in the first six months of 1916.

Section 4. Ground-wood costs, 1913–1916.

All of the companies operating news-print mills included in Table 16 operate one or more ground-wood mills, and Table 23 shows the average cost of production of ground wood for the United States mills, for Canadian mills, and for the United States and Canadian mills combined.

TABLE 23.—AVERAGE COST OF MANUFACTURE PER TON OF GROUND WOOD FOR UNITED STATES AND CANADIAN MILLS, 1913-1916 (FIRST HALF).

Item.	United States.				Canada.				United States and Canada combined.			
	1913	1914	1915	First half 1916.	1913	1914	1915	First half 1916.	1913	1914	1915	First half 1916.
Number of mills	45	50	50	47	7	10	11	10	52	60	61	57
Tons produced	698,222	770,017	844,815	511,243	216,151	328,460	406,960	187,707	914,373	1,098,478	1,251,775	698,950
Stock:												
Wood	$9.51	$9.32	$9.57	$9.41	$7.03	$7.30	$7.34	$7.45	$8.92	$8.72	$8.85	$8.88
Conversion:												
Labor	2.43	2.36	2.18	2.05	1.66	1.71	1.55	1.20	2.25	2.16	1.98	1.82
Stones	.12	.14	.12	.11	.11	.09	.08	.13	.12	.13	.11	.12
Felts	.08	.08	.09	.09	.08	.07	.05	.04	.08	.08	.07	.07
Wires	.03	.03	.03	.04	.02	.02	.02	.02	.03	.02	.03	.04
Belting	.07	.07	.05	.05	.05	.03	.04	.03	.06	.06	.05	.04
Lubricants	.03	.03	.03	.02	.03	.03	.03	.02	.03	.03	.02	.02
Repairs	.91	.87	.78	.65	.44	.48	.43	.38	.80	.76	.67	.60
Power and water rentals	.54	.58	.57	.52	.49	.53	.53	.50	.53	.56	.55	.51
Miscellaneous	.28	.31	.31	.31	.31	.29	.33	.25	.29	.30	.32	.30
Total	4.49	4.47	4.16	3.87	3.19	3.25	3.05	2.58	4.19	4.10	3.80	3.52
General expense:												
Taxes and insurance	.30	.28	.23	.22	.12	.13	.12	.10	.25	.24	.19	.19
Administrative	.33	.39	.33	.27	.44	.37	.37	.41	.36	.38	.34	.31
Total	.63	.67	.56	.49	.56	.50	.49	.51	.61	.62	.53	.50
Total cost [1]	14.63	14.46	14.29	13.77	10.78	11.05	10.89	10.54	13.72	13.44	13.18	12.90

[1] Exclusive of depreciation which on the average would be about $0.55 per ton of ground wood.

These average costs are shown by items for the years 1913, 1914, 1915, and the first six months of 1916. The costs do not include a depreciation charge which, as noted in section 1, is charged to the news-print paper in which the ground wood is used.

The table shows but little change in the average cost of manufacturing ground wood between 1913 and the first half of 1916. Although the same number of mills is not included in each year, the relation between the costs for the various years would not change materially by making the figures strictly comparable in this regard.

The cost of pulp wood is the most important item, and it should be noted that much of this material used in the first half of 1916 was purchased under old contracts made at low prices. The next most important item in cost per ton is labor, which in general showed a downward trend per ton both in the United States and in Canada. This was no doubt due chiefly to the increased output of the mills.

The cost of producing ground wood has been higher in the United States than in Canada, the difference in the first six months of 1916 being $3.23 per ton, this being chiefly due to the difference in the cost of the pulp wood used.

AVERAGE COSTS FOR SECOND HALF OF 1916.—In December, 1916, the Commission secured cost data from 35 mills in the United States covering a part of the period since July 1, 1916. The average period covered by these cost data was about four months but for individual mills ranged from three to five months. These mills during the first half of 1916 produced 75 per cent of the total tonnage included in the tables. These figures have not been revised and are compared only with the average costs as shown on the books of the companies. The average cost of ground wood for all mills in the latter part of 1916 was $1.06 per ton higher than the average cost for the same mills during the first half of the year. The important items which increased were wood, labor, and repairs. The increase in wood costs for the latter part of the year was due to the fact that logging costs had increased and materially higher prices were paid for pulp wood purchased in 1916. Overhead expenses were also slightly higher for the latter period, due to the decrease in output of several of the mills during the summer months.

Additional cost data were secured in February, 1917, from 40 mills in the United States for either the month of December, 1916, or January, 1917. These mills during the first half of 1916 produced 79 per cent of the total tonnage of the mills included. The average cost of ground wood for these mills during this one-month period was $3.13 per ton higher than the unrevised cost for the same mills during the first half of 1916.

PERCENTAGE OF COST.—The importance of pulp wood and various other items of expense included in the cost of producing ground wood is shown by Table 24, which gives the percentage of the total cost attributable to each item for United States and Canadian mills combined for the years 1913 to 1915 and first half of 1916.

TABLE 24.—PERCENTAGE OF TOTAL COST OF PRODUCING GROUND WOOD ATTRIBU-
TABLE TO PARTICULAR ITEMS—UNITED STATES AND CANADIAN MILLS COM-
BINED—1913-1916 (FIRST HALF).

Item.	1913	1914	1915	First half 1916.
	Per cent.	*Per cent.*	*Per cent.*	*Per cent.*
Wood	65.04	61.86	67.11	68.85
Conversion:				
Labor	16.38	16.11	15.00	14.12
Stones	.86	.94	.82	.92
Felts	.57	.57	.55	.57
Wires	.19	.19	.21	.27
Belting	.45	.43	.35	.34
Lubricants	.24	.22	.20	.17
Repairs	5.83	5.62	5.07	4.65
Power and water rentals	3.87	4.21	4.20	3.98
Miscellaneous	2.11	2.25	2.43	2.28
Total	30.50	30.54	28.83	27.30
General expense:				
Taxes and insurance	1.86	1.78	1.46	1.49
General and administrative	2.60	2.82	2.60	2.36
Total	4.46	4.60	4.06	3.85
Total cost[1]	100.00	100.00	100.00	100.00

[1] Exclusive of depreciation.

The cost of wood was the chief item, representing 69 per cent of the total cost in the first half of 1916 and 65 per cent in 1913. Next in importance in 1916 came labor (14 per cent) and repairs (4.6 per cent). Felts, wires, and belting taken together made less than 2 per cent of the total cost per ton of ground wood.

AVERAGE COST OF PRODUCING GROUND WOOD, BY GROUPS OF MILLS.—The differences in the cost of production of the domestic ground-wood mills included in the table of average costs above are shown by Table 25 following, which groups the mills into five classes and shows the number included, the tonnage represented, the percentage of the total tonnage, and the average cost per ton for each group for the years 1913, 1914, 1915, and the first half of 1916.

TABLE 25.—COST OF PRODUCTION OF GROUND WOOD IN UNITED STATES MILLS COVERED BY THE INVESTIGATION, ARRANGED BY GROUPS ACCORDING TO COST PER TON, 1913-1916 (FIRST HALF).

Group.	Number of mills.	Produced.	Per cent of total.	Average cost per ton.[1]
1913.		Tons.		
I (less than $10.50)...............................	1	75,990	10.9	$10.37
II ($10.50 and less than $12.50).......................	3	100,346	14.4	10.99
III ($12.50 and less than $15)........................	12	193,320	27.7	13.94
IV ($15 and less than $17)...........................	15	184,970	26.5	16.13
V ($17 and over)....................................	14	143,596	20.5	18.40
Total...	45	698,222	100.0	14.63
1914.				
I (less than $10.50)................................	1	88,584	11.5	10.40
II ($10.50 and less than $12.50)......................	4	137,689	17.9	10.97
III ($12.50 and less than $15)........................	13	127,475	16.5	14.23
IV ($15 and less than $17)...........................	21	290,257	37.7	15.79
V ($17 and over)....................................	11	126,012	16.4	18.29
Total...	50	770,017	100.0	14.40
1915.				
I (less than $10.50)................................				
II ($10.50 and less than $12.50)......................	5	223,777	26.5	11.23
III ($12.50 and less than $15)........................	21	370,896	43.9	14.23
IV ($15 and less than $17)...........................	13	160,995	19.1	16.11
V ($17 and over)....................................	11	89,147	10.5	18.88
Total...	50	844,815	100.0	14.29
1916 (first half).				
I (less than $10.50)................................				
II ($10.50 and less than $12.50)......................	7	175,339	34.3	11.29
III ($12.50 and less than $15.).......................	21	209,963	41.1	14.04
IV ($15 and less than $17)...........................	12	89,736	17.5	15.97
V ($17 and over)....................................	7	36,205	7.1	18.69
Total...	47	511,243	100.0	13.77

[1] Exclusive of depreciation.

The table shows that the percentage of ground wood produced by United States mills having a cost of over $17 per ton decreased during the three and one-half year period. The decrease from 10.5 per cent to 7.1 per cent between 1915 and the first half of 1916, however, might be reduced by the inclusion of mills for which data were not available for the latter period.

Section 5. News-print paper profits per ton.

Table 26 below shows what changes have taken place in the profits per ton of news-print paper sold since 1913, together with the cost of sales and net selling prices for the same mills in Canada and the United States from which the cost figures shown in preceding sections for news print, sulphite, and ground wood were obtained.

TABLE 26.—AVERAGE SALES, COSTS, AND PROFITS PER TON OF NEWS-PRINT PAPER FOR UNITED STATES AND CANADIAN MILLS, 1913-1916 (FIRST HALF).

Item.	United States.				Canada.				United States and Canada combined.			
	1913	1914	1915	First half 1916	1913	1914	1915	First half 1916	1913	1914	1915	First half 1916
Number of mills	30	35	35	34	7	9	11	10	37	44	46	44
Tons sold	951,057	1,065,628	1,047,427	546,436	215,930	348,926	431,763	221,704	1,166,987	1,414,554	1,479,190	768,140
Gross sales	$43.75	$42.88	$42.49	$43.43	$43.46	$42.46	$41.65	$42.21	$43.70	$42.77	$42.25	$43.08
Deductions for discount, cartage, freight, etc.	4.25	4.12	4.04	4.03	5.32	4.75	4.31	4.28	4.45	4.28	4.12	4.10
Net sales	39.50	38.76	38.45	39.40	38.14	37.71	37.34	37.95	39.25	38.49	38.13	38.98
Cost of sales	33.36	33.21	32.22	32.06	30.83	30.13	28.19	27.45	32.89	32.44	31.04	30.73
Selling expenses	.61	.61	.64	.59	.86	.96	1.02	.97	.66	.70	.75	.70
Total	33.97	33.82	32.86	32.65	31.69	31.09	29.21	28.42	33.55	33.14	31.79	31.43
Profits	5.53	4.94	5.59	6.75	6.45	6.62	8.13	9.54	5.70	5.35	6.34	7.55
Per cent of profits on net sales	14.00	12.75	14.56	17.12	16.91	17.55	21.77	25.15	14.52	13.91	16.62	19.38

The table shows the average results for United States mills and Canadian mills, and for United States and Canadian mills combined, for the years 1913, 1914, 1915, and the first half of 1916. The table shows the tons sold and gross receipts per ton, the total amount of deductions per ton from gross receipts for discounts and allowances, freight, storage, and cartage, and the net sales per ton resulting from such deductions, the cost of sales per ton including general expense and depreciation, which is the total cost of manufacture with inventory adjustments, selling expenses per ton, profits per ton, and the percentage of profits to net sales.

The average gross receipts per ton for the varying groups of United States mills were lowest in 1915 at $42.49 per ton and highest in 1913 at $43.75 per ton. The gross receipts for the groups of Canadian mills covered in the table were slightly lower, ranging from $41.65 per ton in 1915 to $43.46 per ton in 1913. The total deductions from gross receipts necessary to arrive at net receipts for the United States mills showed a downward trend during the period, ranging from $4.25 per ton in 1913 to $4.03 in the first half of 1916. The total deductions for Canadian mills were slightly higher, ranging from $5.32 in 1913 to $4.28 in the first half of 1916. This was probably due to the higher freight rates from Canadian mills to the United States market. Net receipts for the United States mills declined from $39.50 per ton in 1913 to $38.45 per ton in 1915, and then rose to $39.40 per ton in the first half of 1916. Likewise, net receipts for the Canadian mills declined from $38.14 in 1913 to $37.34 in 1915, and then rose to $37.96 per ton in the first half of 1916. The net receipts for the United States mills and Canadian mills combined declined from $39.25 per ton in 1913 to $38.13 in 1915 and then rose to $38.98 in the first half of 1916.

The cost of sales, including general expenses, for Canadian mills and United States and Canadian mills combined, declined during the three and one-half year period in the same manner as the cost of manufacture shown in section 2. The cost of sales for Canadian mills in the first half of 1916 was $4.60 less than the cost of sales for United States mills.

Selling expenses for United States mills were lowest in the first half of 1916 at 59 cents per ton and highest in 1915 at 64 cents per ton. For Canadian mills selling expenses were highest in 1915 at $1.02 per ton and lowest in 1913 at 86 cents per ton. The higher selling expense for Canadian mills was probably due to the fact that most of them sell through brokers and selling agents instead of maintaining their own selling organization.

The average profit per ton for the United States mills included in the table was lowest in 1914 at $4.94 and highest in the first half of 1916 at $6.75 per ton. The average profit per ton for Canadian mills showed a steady increase during the three and one-half year period, the lowest being $6.45 in 1913 and the highest $9.54 per ton in the first half of 1916. This was an increase of $3.09 per ton over the profit in 1913 and $2.79 per ton higher than the profit for United States mills in the first half of 1916. Combining the United States and Canadian mills, the average profit per ton was lowest in 1914 at $5.35 and highest in the first half of 1916 at $7.55.

The percentage of profit on net sales for United States mills ranged from 12.8 per cent in 1914 to 17.1 per cent in the first half of 1916. The percentage of profit on net sales for Canadian mills ranged from 16.9 per cent in 1913 to 25.2 per cent in the first half of 1916. For the United States and Canadian mills combined the percentage of profit on net sales ranged from 13.9 per cent in 1914 to 19.4 per cent in the first half of 1916. The rate of profit on investment is shown below. (See p. 110.)

As is the case with the cost tables in preceding sections, the profit figures for each year are not strictly comparable with respect to the number of mills included in the averages. This may explain, in part at least, the decline in profits per ton of United States mills in 1914. The relation between the profits for 1915 and the first half of 1916, however, is not materially affected by the difference in the number of mills included.

AVERAGE PROFITS OF UNITED STATES MILLS, BY GROUPS.—The differences in the profits per ton of United States mills are shown in Table 27 below, which classifies the various mills into six groups and shows for each the number of mills included, the tonnage represented, the percentage of the total tonnage sold, and the average profit per ton for the years 1913, 1914, 1915, and first half of 1916. Mills showing a loss are included in Group VI.

TABLE 27.—VARIATIONS IN THE PROFITS PER TON OF NEWS-PRINT PAPER SOLD BY UNITED STATES MILLS COVERED BY THE INVESTIGATION, BY GROUPS, 1913-1916 (FIRST HALF).

Group.	Number of mills.	Tons sold.	Per cent of total sales.	Average profit per ton.
1913.				
I (($12 and over))	1	65,435	6.9	$12.00
II ($10 and less than $12)	2	125,783	13.2	10.43
III ($8 and less than $10)	1	42,156	4.4	9.81
IV ($6 and less than $8)	4	141,981	14.9	7.14
V ($4 and less than $6)	8	232,144	24.3	4.73
VI (Less than $4)	14	346,558	36.3	1.90
Total	30	954,057	100.0	5.53
1914.				
I ($12 and over)				
II ($10 and less than $12)	2	188,083	17.7	10.15
III ($8 and less than $10)	1	58,694	5.5	9.10
IV ($6 and less than $8)	3	160,832	15.1	7.11
V ($4 and less than $6)	5	85,759	8.1	5.61
VI (Less than $4)	24	571,359	53.6	2.07
Total	35	1,065,628	100.0	4.94
1915.				
I ($12 and over)				
II ($10 and less than $12)	1	114,749	11.0	10.37
III ($8 and less than $10)	7	312,457	29.8	9.07
IV ($6 and less than $8)	5	90,493	8.6	6.99
V ($4 and less than $6)	6	169,885	16.2	4.92
VI (Less than $4)	16	359,843	34.4	1.03
Total	35	1,047,427	100.0	5.60
1916 (first half).				
I ($12 and over)	3	58,683	10.7	12.58
II ($10 and less than $12)	4	65,830	12.0	10.74
III ($8 and less than $10)	3	135,202	24.7	9.36
IV ($6 and less than $8)	5	68,999	12.6	6.87
V ($4 and less than $6)	7	74,728	13.8	4.64
VI (Less than $4)	12	142,994	26.2	1.08
Total	34	546,436	100.0	6.75

The above table shows that in 1913 the range of profits by groups was from $12 per ton, high, for one mill to $1.90 per ton, low, for 14 mills combined. Two mills included in Group VI showed a loss of about 28 cents per ton. The average profit for all 30 mills was $5.53 per ton. Of the total tonnage included, 39.4 per cent was sold at an average profit of more than $6 per ton, while 36.3 per cent was sold at a profit of less than $4 per ton.

The range of profit by groups in 1914 was from $10.15 per ton for 2 mills to $2.07 per ton for 24 mills combined in Group VI. The highest profit for an individual mill was $10.35 per ton, while of the mills included in Group VI 5 operated at a loss, the loss in 1 mill being as much as $1.94 per ton. The average profit for all 35 mills was $4.94 per ton. Of the total tonnage, 38.3 per cent was sold at an average profit exceeding $6 per ton, while 53.6 per cent was sold at a profit of less than $4 per ton.

In 1915 the average profit by groups ranged from $10.37 per ton for 1 mill to $1.03 per ton for 16 mills. Of the mills included in the latter group, 5 showed a loss during the year. The highest individual profit for any mill was $10.37 per ton, while 1 mill showed a loss of $7.19 per ton. Of the total tonnage represented, 49.4 per cent was sold at an average profit of above $6 per ton, while 34.4 per cent was sold at an average of less than $4 per ton. The average profits for any mill did not exceed $12 per ton in 1914 or 1915.

In the first half of 1916 the range of profit by groups was from $12.58 per ton for 3 mills combined to $1.08 per ton for 12 mills. Of the mills included in the latter group, 3 showed a loss. The average loss in 1 mill was $6.30 per ton. The highest profit shown in any individual mill was $13.08 per ton. The average profit for all 34 mills was $6.75 per ton, or $1.15 per ton more than in 1915. Of the total tonnage, 60 per cent was sold at an average profit exceeding $6 per ton, while 26.2 per cent was sold at a profit of less than $4 per ton.

If the Canadian mills were classified in the same manner, 1 would have been included in Group I, in 1913, 4 in Group IV, and 2 in Group VI. In 1914, of the 9 mills whose average profit was $6.62 per ton, 1 would have been included in Group I, 1 in Group III, 2 each in Groups IV and V, and 3 in Group VI. In 1915, of the 11 Canadian mills with an average profit of $8.13 per ton, 2 would have been included in Group I, 1 in Group III, 5 in Group IV, 2 in Group V, and 1 in Group VI. In the first half of 1916, of the 10 mills with an average profit of $9.55 per ton, 2 would have been included in Group I, 1 in Group II, 4 in Group III, 1 in Group IV, and 2 in Group VI. The average profits for Canadian mills covered by the investigation in the first half of 1916 exceeded the average profits in 1915 by $1.42 per ton.

The average profit of 15 additional mills in the United States not included in the profit tables above, from which data were obtained largely by correspondence without revision by the Commission, was only 56 cents per ton in 1915. If grouped according to the classification shown in Table 27, 1 mill would fall in Group V and 14 in Group VI, 5 of which showed a loss in this year. In the first half of 1916 the average profit for these mills as reported to the Commission had increased to $2.35 per ton. Classified by groups, 1 mill would fall in Group IV, 1 in Group V, and 12 in Group VI. Only 1 mill of this group of 15, however, showed a loss in this half year.

These 15 additional mills have a combined tonnage representing a little less than 13 per cent of the total domestic production. If they were included in the table of average profits per ton, the figures for 1915 and the first half of 1916 would represent about 95 per cent and 93 per cent, respectively, of the total domestic production. The average profit per ton, including these mills, would be $4.94 in 1915 and $6.15 in the first half of 1916.

Section 6. Profits on investment.

The Commission found it impracticable in some cases and impossible in others to determine the actual cost of investment of the properties of domestic news-print companies, which is the only true basis for reckoning the rates of profit. Many of the companies have been reorganized, and the original records are not obtainable, and in others, in order to arrive at the original cost of the properties acquired, it would have been necessary to examine the financial statements of the companies for several years. It was also found impracticable to separate the investment in the news-print branch of the business from the total investment. The total revised earnings, therefore, are compared with the total net book investment, after making such revisions as the available information permitted.

Comparable financial statements were secured from 15 companies in the United States for the years 1915 and 1916. The total net book investment of these companies in 1915 was about $140,000,000, while the investment as revised by the Commission was about $116,000,000. The companies included produced in 1915 about 90 per cent of the tonnage represented in the cost tables and about 75 per cent of the total production in the United States.

The total net book investment is obtained by combining the book value of the real estate, buildings, equipment, etc., incidental to the paper and pulp mills, the book value of the timberlands and water-power properties, and the working capital (accounts and bills receivable and cash less bills and accounts payable) as carried on the books of the companies. Investments in sawmills, industrial railroads, etc., are also included, since the total earnings of the companies are included. Where a reserve for depreciation was made this amount has been deducted, since a liberal charge for depreciation has been allowed in costs.

The Commission has revised the book investment of certain of these companies where information obtained showed inflations in capital. For example, it was admitted by an officer of one large company that the original common stock of his company did not represent tangible property. In other cases it was apparent that the investment in timberlands or water-power properties had been written up, while one company carried an item of good will on its books which did not represent any investment cost.

Table 28 below gives the rates of profit on the net book investment as shown by the companies and on the net investment as revised by the Commission for the year 1915 and the first half of 1916.

TABLE 28.—RATES OF PROFIT ON NET INVESTMENT OF 15 UNITED STATES COMPANIES, 1915-1916 (FIRST HALF).

[Revised earnings are compared with net investment as shown by the books and with net investment, as revised by the Commission.]

Company.	1915		First half 1916.[1]	
	On investment as shown by books.	On investment as revised by Commission.	On investment as shown by books.	On investment as revised by Commission.
1........................	*2.4	*2.4	*2.6	*2.6
2........................	8.1	10.8	11.9	15.8
3........................	*11.9	*11.9	14.4	14.4
4........................	9.0	9.0	19.3	19.3
5........................	1.1	1.1	6.0	6.0
6........................	5.0	5.0	7.6	7.6
7........................	12.1	12.1	23.0	23.0
8........................	8.8	6.8	8.6	8.6
9........................	5.2	8.0	4.9	7.5
10.......................	13.5	13.5	11.8	11.8
11.......................	3.8	5.2	*6.0	*8.2
12.......................	6.8	8.5	11.6	14.5
13.......................	2.0	2.0	9.4	9.4
14.......................	1.5	1.5	5.5	5.5
15.......................	11.2	11.2	11.6	11.6
All companies combined........	5.4	6.5	7.9	9.5

[1] Annual rate for the 6-months' period of 1916 is shown

[2] Figures in italics indicate losses.

[3] Earnings of this company for the first half of 1916 include no revenue from sources other than mill operations. This revenue in 1916 was about 0.7 per cent on the company's entire investment. Depreciation and bond interest were computed on basis of the year 1915.

The revised rate of profit for the 15 companies combined was 6.5 per cent in 1915 and at the annual rate of 9.5 per cent in the first half of 1916. The corresponding rates on the investment shown by the books were 5.4 in 1915 and at the annual rate of 7.9 per cent in the first half of 1916.

The rate of earnings of the individual companies on the investment as revised by the Commission ranged in 1915 from a loss of 11.9 per cent for 1 company to a profit of 13.5 per cent for another company, and exceeded 8 per cent in the case of 8 of the 15 companies. In the first half of 1916 the rate of earnings based on the revised investment ranged from a loss of 2.6 per cent for one company to a profit of 23 per cent for another company. The rate of profit exceeded 8 per cent in the case of 10 companies during this year.

The average rates of profit on investment in 1915 and in the first half of 1916 (6.5 per cent and 9.5 per cent, respectively, as revised by the Commission) are the rates earned on the companies' entire business, including paper other than news print. An analysis of the earnings, taking into account the fact that the 1916 figures cover only six months, shows that the 50 per cent increase was due to an increase of 20 per cent in news print earnings and of 192 per cent on other business. As the profits per ton realized on some other grades of paper were higher than on news print, the rates shown in the table, especially in 1916, are above those actually attributable to news print paper alone.

From the foregoing data it is apparent that, on the average, net earnings in the news print business in 1915 were comparatively low. However, it is probable that the rates of profit, if based on the actual cost of investment, would be somewhat higher than those shown in the table. The net book investment, excluding outside investments, averaged about $35,000 per ton of daily output, and on the revised investment about $30,000 per ton of daily output. The Tariff Board, in its report [1] on the industry, stated that for an investment for power and fully equipped and balanced plant $17,000 to $20,000 per ton of daily output should be taken as a liberal estimate. To this, however, must be added provision for working capital and woodlands, which brings the total estimated investment up to between $25,000 and $30,000 per ton of daily output. According to statements made by manufacturers and opinions of experts, such an allowance for a well-balanced mill, including working capital and necessary woodlands, is ample. On the $25,000 basis the average rates of profit shown in Table 28 for total operations of 15 companies would have been about 7.5 per cent in 1915 and about 11.5 per cent in the first half of 1916. On the news print operations of these companies alone the rate of profit in the first half of 1916 could hardly have been as much as 10 per cent even on the $25,000 basis. Furthermore, available information that is not of a comparable character indicates that the average rate of profit realized by the entire domestic news print industry was somewhat less than is shown in Table 28.

In this connection the effect of the advance in prices of news print should be noted. Both in 1915 and the first half of 1916 there were 24 mills in the United States which were making 85 per cent of the total domestic output at costs varying, in round numbers, from $25 to $35 per ton. The bulk of their output is now being sold on annual contracts at prices ranging from $60 to $70 per ton. Evidently

---

[1] Pulp and News Print Paper Industry; S. Doc. 31, 62d Cong., 1st sess., p. 73.

such prices provide a margin of $25 to $45 per ton over the above costs. This margin, of course, must take care of increased costs before any increase in profits is obtained. Costs have increased in a few peculiarly unfortunate mills as much as $15 per ton. An increase of that amount in all of the 24 mills is practically impossible unless some unforeseen calamity changes the situation entirely. But even for the high cost mills present prices provide a margin of profit of from $10 to $30 per ton as compared with the margins of $4.94 to $6.75 per ton shown in Table 26.

Further, it should be noted that under normal conditions each dollar added to the net margin between cost and price adds about 1 per cent to the rate of profit on an investment of $30,000 per ton of daily output. Consequently, even if there should be a general increase in costs of $15 per ton, these mills, without pushing their machines above a normal output, would, at present prices, realize profits ranging from 10 per cent to more than 30 per cent on investment.

Section 7. Conclusions.

There was no marked change in the average cost of producing news-print paper in the United States and Canada during the period from January 1, 1913, to June 30, 1916, covered by the Commission's investigation. The prevailing impression that this cost had increased considerably in the first half of 1916 was chiefly due to the much advertised increase in wages and the high market prices of some of the materials necessary to the manufacture of news print.[1] Account was not taken of the fact that a large part of the actual cost of making the paper, even in the last half of 1916, was determined by contracts signed, wages paid, and expenses incurred in 1914 and 1915, when prices were at their lowest ebb. Most of the pulp wood used in 1916 was cut during the two preceding years and most of the sulphite purchased in 1916 by mills not having their own digesters was on contracts at 1915 prices. The same was generally true of coal and other materials. The cost in 1916, as shown by the accounts, was also kept down by making a paper that contained a smaller proportion of the relatively expensive materials, such as sulphite, colors, and chemicals, than had been used formerly. The greatly increased production also tended to reduce the cost per ton for various items of expense.

The limited investigation which the Commission was able to make of conditions in the last half of 1916 showed that current high costs of materials and labor were beginning to increase the average cost of producing news print. Nevertheless, it does not appear probable

---

[1] The details regarding the increased cost propaganda promoted by the News-Print Manufacturers Association are discussed elsewhere (see Chap. VII).

that the increase in cost for the last half of the year over the first could generally have exceeded $2 to $4 per ton of paper.

The Commission does not attempt to forecast the future course of news print costs. Certain important factors affecting it, however, should be considered. The high cost of labor and materials is already in effect in many mills. In others it has only recently begun to show in the cost of the finished paper; but in mills producing a considerable part of the total product it will probably not reach its full effect before new low cost factors such as increased number of domestic pulp mills and increasing imports of foreign pulp will have reduced costs in the present high cost mills.

It does not appear that the average cost of news-print paper will advance to a level corresponding to the spot prices of its constituent elements during 1916, unless very abnormal and unexpected conditions develop.

Two points affecting news-print manufacturers in the United States should be pointed out: First, the cost of news print in Canada, which covers about 26 per cent of the total supply of the United States, is from $4 to $5 less per ton than in this country. Second, some of the large publishers are already making their own news print, and it is probable that others of equal financial ability will build mills rather than for any length of time pay prices in excess of cost of production plus a fair return on investment.

The prices made by the manufacturers at the end of 1916 did not take full account of the situation as outlined above. It is clear that the open-market prices during the last two or three months in 1916, and from then to the present time, have in many cases been extortionate. The contract prices charged many newspapers, especially the smaller daily and weekly publications, have also been excessively high. Such prices have in not a few cases been over $75 a ton and have ranged as high as $100 and $110. A comparison of advances in price with advances in cost of production shows an enhancement in the former much greater than the increase in the latter.

These excessively high prices ignored the public interest, which requires the maintenance of news-print prices both on a reasonable level and, except for reasonable differences in quantity, freight, etc., on a parity between different publishers. It appears, moreover, that these prices, in opposition to the long-time interests of the manufacturers themselves, tended to increase investment in news-print manufacture by newspaper publishers, to increase competition from abroad, and to cause the immediate use of pulp-wood reserves that would not, at lower prices, be thrown upon the market during 1917.

The prices of $65 per ton or more on contracts made with larger newspapers toward the end of 1916, and now being charged, are also excessively high in comparison with costs, if a few mills of small tonnage and exceptionally high costs are left out of consideration. It should be emphasized that, in such times of abnormal costs and prices, panic demand, and temporary decline in stocks, the exaction of long-term contracts at inflexible prices is not only contrary to the public interest but is also unreasonable from a business standpoint. With the restoration of more normal conditions such terms are almost certain to become unreasonable to the purchaser. If, on the other hand, costs were to increase further than anticipated or a scarcity arise the seller might be injured. Under the existing circumstances the best arrangement would be to make contracts on a sliding scale based on cost, provided the base price were fair and the terms of the contract were otherwise reasonable.

At least two companies, one of which has a very large production, have generally refused to follow the excessive prices now often charged, and have contracted to sell most of their 1917 production for from $10 to $18 per ton below the most usual contract price of $65. They have apparently acted according to their best business judgment and have refused to take advantage of the extreme necessity of their customers for the purpose of exacting the highest possible price.

In the Commission's judgment the present prices of news-print paper are above what is requisite for a profitable development of the industry. It is clear, therefore, that they can not be long maintained except by a monopolistic control of the market.

CHAPTER VI.

SUPPLY AND DEMAND FACTORS.

Section 1. Introduction.

This chapter presents the information collected by the Commission with respect to the demand for news-print paper in 1916 as compared with prior years and the supply available to satisfy this demand.

Business prosperity in the United States in 1916 caused an unusual domestic demand not only for news-print paper but for all grades of paper, and the European war, by curtailing the production abroad, caused an increased demand by foreign buyers in the markets of the United States and Canada. The result was a considerable increase in domestic consumption and a relatively large increase in exports.

The output of United States mills which, as shown in Chapter II, declined in 1914 and 1915, showed a considerable increase in 1916, and the output of Canadian mills, most of which is sold in the United States, showed a large increase in 1916 over 1915, resulting in greatly increased exports to this country. It appears, however, that the increase in the supply coming from United States and Canadian mills was not sufficient to meet the combined domestic and foreign demand, for stocks on hand declined almost steadily throughout the year 1916. The changes which occurred in production, imports, exports, and stocks on hand during the years 1915 and 1916 are shown by Table 29, following.

TABLE 29.—STATISTICS OF PRODUCTION, IMPORTS, EXPORTS AND STOCKS OF NEWS-PRINT PAPER IN THE UNITED STATES, 1915-1916.

Items.	1915			1916			Per cent of increase of year 1916 over 1915.
	First half.	Second half.	Entire year.	First half.	Second half.[1]	Entire year.	
	Tons.	Tons.	Tons.	Tons.	Tons.	Tons.	
Stocks at beginning of period....	91,650	77,524	91,650	68,912	58,572	68,912	....
Domestic production...........	608,235	630,887	1,239,122	673,737	681,459	1,355,196	9.4
Imports......................	166,842	201,567	368,409	237,179	231,051	468,230	27.1
Total....................	866,727	909,978	1,699,181	979,828	971,082	1,892,338	11.4
Exports.....................	25,752	29,410	55,162	34,213	42,115	76,328	38.4
Available for consumption	840,975	880,568	1,644,019	945,615	928,967	1,816,010	10.5
Stocks at end of period.........	77,524	68,912	68,912	58,572	42,432	42,432	....
Indicated consumption...	763,451	811,656	1,575,107	887,043	886,535	1,773,578	12.6

[1] December figures for production and stocks estimated.

The table shows that domestic production increased during each half-year period, beginning with the middle of 1915. The increase for the year 1916 over 1915 was 9.4 per cent. Imports also showed large increases for each half-year period, the increase in 1916 over 1915 being 27.1 per cent. Exports showed an even greater relative increase, the quantity exported in 1916 being 38.4 per cent greater than in 1915. This was only 5.6 per cent of the domestic production, however, as compared with 4.5 per cent in 1915. Stocks on hand decreased from 91,650 tons at the beginning of the year 1915 to 42,432 tons at the close of the year 1916, a total decrease of 49,218 tons in two years. The increase in the indicated consumption in 1916 over 1915 was 198,471 tons, or 12.6 per cent. This increase was about double the normal annual increase, which is estimated at 6 per cent. Information obtained by the Commission indicates that neither the domestic nor the foreign demand was entirely satisfied by the quantity consumed or exported.

The percentage of increase of the indicated consumption by half-year periods was as follows:

	Per cent.
Second half of 1915 over first half of 1915	6. 3
First half of 1916 over second half of 1915	9. 3
First half of 1916 over first half of 1915	16. 2

The indicated consumption for the second half of 1916 was very nearly the same as for the first half. Reports furnished the Commission by 92 large daily papers showed that their receipts of paper on contract during the first half of 1916 were about 13 per cent greater than for the first half of 1915. In addition, some of them purchased considerable quantities in the open market, which would probably bring the increase in receipts up to the 16 per cent shown above.

Reports of shipments to customers on contract, obtained from the principal news-print manufacturers of the United States and Canada, show that 323 newspapers consumed more than 50 per cent of the total indicated domestic consumption in each half-year period since July 1, 1915. The following tabulation gives the figures in detail:

Period.	Shipments to 323 papers.	Total indicated consumption.	Per centage of total.
	Tons.	Tons.	
1915, second half	435,360	811,656	53. 6
1916:			
First half	473,098	887,043	53. 3
Second half	454,999	888,535	51. 3

The tabulation shows an increase in shipments to the 323 papers for the first half of 1916 over the preceding half-year period of nearly 9 per cent. This is about the percentage of increase for the indicated consumption as shown above. The shipments by mills to these 323 publications show a falling off of about 18,000 tons during the second half of 1916, while the total indicated consumption during the second half of 1916 was approximately equal to that of the first half. This is probably explained by the fact that in the second half of 1916 the 323 publishers bought more paper in the open market than they did in the first half, either because the mill shipments did not meet their requirements or their contracts had expired and were not renewed.

Section 2. Causes of domestic demand.

The increased demand by newspaper publishers in the United States in 1916 was due both to an increase in circulation and to an increase in the number of pages per issue. The increase in circulation resulted partly from the interesting character of the news during the year, there being an unusually large number of important news subjects, such as the European war, Mexican troubles, railroad strikes, presidential campaign, etc. The increase in the number of pages per issue was due to enlarged space for both reading matter and advertising matter but the latter seems to have been the more important cause. Reports from newspapers indicate that the prosperity of the country in 1916 was accompanied by a very large increase in the demand for advertising space.

In addition to the demand from newspaper publishers there was also an increased demand for paper for commercial purposes, and a substitution of news print for book paper by some magazines and periodicals, because of the greatly increased cost of book paper.

The domestic demand for news print paper in 1916 was intensified by the development of a virtual panic among publishers who were not protected by contract in their requirements, so that it gave the appearance of being much greater than it really was.

INCREASE IN CIRCULATION.—The growth in circulation of newspapers is shown by Table 30 below, compiled from sworn returns of 124 daily newspapers to the Post Office Department. The figures shown represent the average daily paid circulation for six months' periods from April 1, 1913, to October 1, 1916, and include newspapers with a circulation of 50,000 or more published in cities of 100,000 population or over, which have furnished statements for the entire period. One hundred and fourteen of these publications were in the English language and 10 in foreign languages. The figures for 44 of the papers include Sunday issues. The percentages of increase are based upon the average daily circulation for the period ending April 1, 1913.

TABLE 30.—AVERAGE DAILY CIRCULATION OF 114 NEWSPAPERS IN ENGLISH AND 10 IN FOREIGN LANGUAGES WITH A CIRCULATION EXCEEDING 50,000 COPIES, 1913-1916.

Six months' period ending—	Total English and foreign.		Total 114 English.		Total 10 foreign.	
	Circulation.	Per cent of increase over six months' period ending Apr. 1, 1913.	Circulation.	Per cent of increase over six months' period ending Apr. 1, 1913.	Circulation.	Per cent of increase over six months' period ending Apr. 1, 1913.
Apr. 1, 1913..............	13,185,708	....	12,599,073	....	586,635	....
Oct. 1, 1913..............	13,445,022	2.0	12,848,063	2.0	596,959	1.8
Apr. 1, 1914..............	13,700,957	3.9	12,959,978	2.9	740,979	26.3
Oct. 1, 1914..............	14,815,094	12.4	13,957,128	10.8	857,966	46.3
Apr. 1, 1915..............	14,872,576	12.8	13,878,557	10.2	994,019	69.4
Oct. 1, 1915..............	15,371,809	16.6	14,379,881	14.1	991,928	69.1
Apr. 1, 1916..............	15,335,885	16.3	14,372,351	14.1	963,534	64.2
Oct. 1, 1916..............	15,969,150	21.1	14,989,007	19.0	980,143	67.1

The table shows that the average daily circulation of the 114 newspapers printed in English showed the greatest increases during the 6-month periods from April to October of each year. The changes in circulation of these papers from October 1 to April 1 were not important. The greatest increase, which occurred in 1914, amounted to 7.7 per cent, as compared with 3.6 per cent in 1915 and 4.3 per cent in 1916.

The average daily circulation of the 10 newspapers printed in foreign languages showed remarkable increases during each 6-months' period until April 1, 1915. During the two following periods there was a falling off of 3.1 per cent, while in the last period there was a gain of 1.7 per cent.

The increase in daily circulation of the 124 daily newspapers included in the table for the 6-months' period ending October 1, 1916, over the preceding period was 633,265 copies, which represents an increase in consumption of, roughly, 20,000 tons per year if it is assumed that the average size of these papers was 14 pages. If the average size was 16 pages, the increase in consumption would amount to about 23,000 tons.

In addition to the 124 daily newspapers shown in the table, there are about 2,300 other daily papers whose average daily circulation would probably be about 7,000 copies. No attempt has been made to ascertain what the increase in circulation or in the consumption of news-print paper by these newspapers has been.

Table 31, following, classifies the 114 daily papers printed in English and shows the increase in the average daily circulation of each class for the same 6-months' periods:

TABLE 31.—AVERAGE DAILY CIRCULATION OF 114 NEWSPAPERS PRINTED IN ENGLISH GROUPED ACCORDING TO CIRCULATION, 1913-1916.

Six-month period ending—	6 newspapers 400,000 and over.		5 newspapers 300,000 to 400,000.		9 newspapers 200,000 to 300,000.		9 newspapers 150,000 to 200,000.		20 newspapers 100,000 to 150,000.		65 newspapers 50,000 to 100,000.	
	Circulation in thousands.	Increase over 6-month period ending Apr. 1, 1913.	Circulation in thousands.	Increase over 6-month period ending Apr. 1, 1913.	Circulation in thousands.	Increase over 6-month period ending Apr. 1, 1913.	Circulation in thousands.	Increase over 6-month period ending Apr. 1, 1913.	Circulation in thousands.	Increase over 6-month period ending Apr. 1, 1913.	Circulation in thousands.	Increase over 6-month period ending Apr. 1, 1913.
		Per ct.		Per ct.		Per ct.		Per ct.		Per ct.		Per ct.
Apr. 1, 1913....	2,445	......	1,551	......	1,612	......	1,328	......	1,841	......	3,822	......
Oct. 1, 1913.....	2,448	0.1	1,579	1.8	1,622	0.6	1,335	0.5	1,937	5.2	3,927	2.7
Apr. 1, 1914.....	2,502	2.3	1,612	3.9	1,579	¹5.0	1,367	2.9	1,970	7.0	3,930	2.8
Oct. 1, 1914.....	2,665	9.0	1,704	9.9	1,842	14.3	1,432	7.8	2,112	14.7	4,202	9.9
Apr. 1, 1915....	2,660	8.8	1,705	9.9	1,840	14.1	1,418	6.8	2,093	13.7	4,163	8.9
Oct. 1, 1915.....	2,765	13.1	1,703	15.6	1,926	19.5	1,493	12.4	2,235	21.4	4,168	9.1
Apr. 1, 1916....	2,794	14.3	1,781	14.8	1,875	16.3	1,517	14.2	2,234	21.3	4,172	9.2
Oct. 1, 1916.....	2,915	19.2	1,888	21.7	1,980	22.8	1,571	18.3	2,283	24.0	4,353	13.9

¹ Decrease.

The largest increase in circulation since April 1, 1913, amounting to 24 per cent, was shown by the papers between 100,000 and 150,000 copies per day. Those between 200,000 and 300,000 made nearly as great an increase, however. The smallest increase was made by the papers between 50,000 and 100,000 copies.

INCREASE IN ADVERTISING.—The volume of advertising determines to a large extent the size of newspapers and is probably the most important factor affecting the consumption of print paper. Statistics of advertising obtained by the Commission from 101 large daily papers show the following increases in 1916 over 1915:

	Per cent.
January, 1916, over January, 1915	9.3
March, 1916, over March, 1915	11.1
May, 1916, over May, 1915	12.9
June, 1916, over June, 1915	14.8

Published statistics of advertising for the principal daily papers in New York, Philadelphia, Boston, and Chicago for the first half of 1916 also show large increases over the first half and second half of 1915, as Table 32 following indicates.

City.	Number of publications.	Total number of columns of advertising January to June, 1916.	Percentage of increase, January to June, 1916, over—			
			July to December, 1915.	January to June, 1915.	July to December, 1914.	January to June, 1914.
New York..........................	17	231,608	9.1	7.9	16.9	1.0
Boston.............................	9	72,176	19.9	16.1	27.0	8.9
Chicago............................	7	95,719	14.5	12.4	21.0	13.0
Philadelphia.......................	7	94,508	24.4	23.1	....	....
Total............................	40	494,011	14.9	12.6	....	....

[1] Compiled from statistics furnished by one newspaper in each city, except Chicago, for which the statistics were furnished by the Washington Press Co.

Seventeen daily papers in Greater New York had a total of 231,608 columns of advertising during the first six months of 1916, which was 9.1 per cent greater than for the preceding six months and 7.9 per cent greater than for the first half of 1915. Nine Boston papers show an increase in the number of columns of advertising of 19.9 per cent over the second half of 1915 and 16.1 per cent over the first half. Seven Chicago papers show an increase of 14.5 per cent over the second half of 1915 and 12.4 per cent over the first half. Seven Philadelphia papers show an increase of 24.4 per cent over the second half of 1915 and 23.1 per cent over the first half. The 40 daily papers having an aggregate of 494,000 columns of advertising during the first six months of 1916 show an increase of 14.9 per cent over the preceding six months and 12.6 per cent over the first half of 1915.

The increase in the volume of advertising in 1916 shown by the preceding tables necessitated a considerable although not corresponding increase in the size of papers and in the consumption of news-print paper. The increase in the price of paper and the campaigns for curtailing consumption led to the introduction of economies and changes which partially offset the demand for additional advertising space. In some cases the proportion of reading matter to advertising was considerably reduced.

EFFECT OF PANIC CONDITIONS.—Various factors contributed to the creation of a panic among publishers in 1916, which caused a bidding up of prices and gave the appearance of a much greater demand and consequent shortage than actually existed. Trade reports were replete with stories of rapidly increasing costs and declining stocks. Publishers who "went shopping" among manufacturers and jobbers were generally told that the latter had no paper to offer. This

threw them back upon the manufacturer or jobber who had origi-
nally supplied them, who was in a position to charge almost any
price he saw fit. In some cases the publisher could no longer obtain
paper from the original source of supply because the mill had been
sold or the machines had been changed to other grades of paper.
They were thus compelled to canvass every known source of supply
until paper could be found.

When contracts expired the mills in some cases would not renew
them. In other cases, when contracts were renewed, the tonnage
allotted was reduced below the actual requirements of the newspapers, so that they were forced to seek additional supplies in the
open market.

A single publisher in quest of paper sometimes canvassed every
manufacturer within reach and also various jobbers and selling agents,
who in turn canvassed the mills from which they received their supplies, causing a piling up of inquiries for paper which gave the appearance of a greater demand than really existed.

In some cases publishers bought more paper than they actually
needed and stored it as a protection against future shortage and high
prices. The quantity thus stored, however, was probably not large.

Section 3. Causes of foreign demand.

The keen foreign demand for news-print paper in the United States
and Canadian markets has been due to changed conditions abroad resulting from the European war. Before the war Germany, Norway,
and Sweden were exporters of paper and paper materials. Austria
also exported some news print, and Finland supplied Russia. England and France imported pulp and made most of their own paper.
The United States imported considerable quantities of chemical pulp
from Scandinavian countries as well as a few tons of news print. The
European war completely changed these conditions. Germany became an importer of the bulk of Swedish pulp instead of an exporter
of pulp and paper. The supply of Russian pulp wood which Norway
uses in large quantities was cut off. Necessities of war compelled
Great Britain to requisition much merchant tonnage, and consequently shipments of coal to Sweden were restricted. Thereupon, in
January, 1916, Sweden retaliated by declaring a virtual embargo upon
the exportation of chemical pulp to Great Britain. Since Sweden furnished about two-thirds of the consumption of pulp in England,
amounting to 461,219 short tons, a severe shortage occurred in that
country. To make up this deficiency English consumers turned to the
Norwegian product, which soon sold at a premium. English paper
makers also became active buyers of paper and pulp in Canada
and the United States. A similar situation developed in France and
other European countries, resulting in shipments from the United
States to countries which normally never bought in our market.

It is reported that during the year 1916 French buyers tried to purchase 60,000 tons of news print in the United States and Canadian
markets, offering attractive prices, but were unsuccessful. Since the
outbreak of the European war Australia and South America have
also been largely dependent upon American and Canadian sources for
their paper supply.

The foreign demand for news-print paper resulted in a large increase in exports during the year 1916, as shown by Table 29 above.
The total exports, however, only amounted to 5.6 per cent of the
domestic production, as compared with 4.5 per cent for the previous
year. Canadian export statistics show that the quantity of print
paper exported to other countries than the United States was no
greater for the first seven months of 1916 than for the corresponding
months of 1915. There was a large increase in the quantity of chemical pulp, or sulphite, exported to Great Britain, however.

That no greater quantity of paper was exported from the North
American Continent was due to the fact that the output of both
Canadian and United States mills was largely contracted for with
publishers in the United States, and also to the fact that shipping
facilities were lacking and ocean rates and insurance extremely high.
Both France and England are reported to have restricted the quantity of paper imported.

The quantity of news-print paper exported from the United States
and Canada in excess of that required to supply regular contract
customers abroad reduced the supply available for the open market,
and to that extent was a factor in the sharp rise in open-market
prices. The attractive prices offered by foreign buyers, even if they
did not secure paper, also had an important effect upon domestic
prices. When contracts with domestic publishers expired American
manufacturers had the choice of renewing them or of selling the
released tonnage to foreign buyers. The foreign bids, therefore,
proved very effective as a leverage in securing an increase in domestic
prices. Foreign buyers, just as did domestic buyers, sought paper
from all possible sources of supply, which resulted in an accumulation of foreign inquiries at the mills and made the quantity demanded
seem much greater than it really was.

Section 4. Causes of limited supply.

It has already been pointed out that the production of news-print
paper in 1916 did not increase as rapidly as the indicated consumption, while a considerable domestic as well as export demand remained unsatisfied. In spite of the attractive prices offered, the
supply was not sufficient to meet the demand. The principal reason
for this condition was the inadequacy of the existing mill equipment
and the impossibility of installing new equipment immediately.

The information collected by the Commission indicates that almost every available machine in the United States and Canada ran 24 hours a day for six days a week throughout the year 1916. Strikes, breakdowns, fires, and floods diminished the possible output somewhat, but probably to a less extent in 1916 than in 1915. Manufacturers state that their mills were speeded up to the limit of their capacity. During the spring months of 1916, on account of favorable water conditions, a number of domestic mills ran even above their normal rated capacity, which is estimated to be about 93 per cent of the maximum capacity. In June, 1916, the average output of all domestic mills belonging to the News Print Manufacturers' Association was reported as 94.3 per cent of their theoretical maximum capacity. In the same month Canadian mills attained an average of 97.7 per cent of their maximum capacity. It thus appears that the manufacturers, both domestic and Canadian, strove to meet the increasing demand and produced as much paper as their news-print equipment would permit. A further increase in output therefore could only have been obtained by building new mills, adding new machines to existing mills, transferring machines from other grades to news print, or running one or more shifts on Sunday.

According to information obtained by the Commission, it takes at least a year to build and install a Fourdrinier paper machine and to develop the water power and install the complementary equipment for making pulp and preparing it in the beater room. Paper machine manufacturers have stated that in 1916 it took considerably longer than formerly to construct a modern Fourdrinier machine, on account of the large amount of business on hand. The cost was also greater. It was, therefore, impossible to build new mills or install new machines during the year to meet the sudden increase in demand for paper. The three new machines that did begin operations in 1916 were in the process of construction when the unusual demand arose. Two of these belong to the International Paper Co. and one to a Canadian company, the Donnacona Paper Co.

Two new mills and several new machines which were also in the process of construction in 1916 will begin operation in the first half of 1917. The present high prices and large profits are also leading to further developments in the industry not previously contemplated. These will not be available, however, until 1918. (See Ch. II, p. 25.)

The transfer of machines from other grades to news-print paper to a sufficient extent to meet the increased demand was prevented by the increase in the prices of other grades of paper and the higher profits generally obtained from their manufacture and sale. When this matter of transferring machines was taken up with the executive committee of the News Print Manufacturers Association by the Commission the members stated that such a transfer would result in a sacrifice in profits which they could not afford to make.

News-print paper manufacturers also stated that Sunday operation was not possible because of the opposition of the labor unions and also because of the necessity of making repairs. One small mill in Wisconsin, however, did succeed in operating on Sunday for several months.

As heretofore pointed out, the domestic news print industry has not grown since 1910, and the increased consumption of domestic publishers has been supplied more and more by Canadian mills. As a result there was not enough surplus mill capacity in 1916 to meet the expansion in demand which occurred. The lack of development shown by the domestic industry is due to a considerable extent to the higher cost of manufacture and lower profits of most mills as compared with Canadian mills. The spruce pulp wood most accessible to domestic mills in many cases has already been used up and present requirements must be met by supplies brought from longer distances. Some companies are paying freight as high as $4 a cord, which increases the cost of the wood at the mill fully a third. In Canada water power is cheaper than in the United States and timberlands can be obtained on more favorable terms, so that the trend of the industry is inevitably in that direction.

Section 5. Prospective supply and demand for 1917.

The relation between supply and demand for 1917 can only be estimated. Figures furnished the Commission by news print manufacturers indicate that the output of mills on the North American Continent will be approximately as great for 1917 as for the preceding year, since new machines coming in will probably offset the tonnage lost by the transfer of machines from news print to other grades as well as by any disturbances that may occur in production. It is reasonable to assume also that the relation of imports, exports, and stocks on hand to the total will remain approximately the same in 1917 as in the preceding year, so that the quantity of paper available for consumption should be as great. This quantity amounted to 1,816,010 tons in 1916.

In December, 1916, the various newspaper associations were requested by the Commission to furnish estimates of the minimum requirements of their members for 1917 and the extent to which their requirements were assured. The data supplied by publishers' associations and individual publishers, taken in connection with the data furnished by manufacturers, indicated that the minimum requirements of the papers reporting for 1917 were assured except about 130,000 tons. These estimates did not include the requirements of a large number of small papers that did not belong to associations and did not report to the Commission, but the aggregate quantity of paper used by such publishers is small.

The reports of news print manufacturers in the United States made at the same time indicated that after fulfilling their contracts and after taking care of those customers that they felt under moral obligations to supply with paper during the first half of 1917, they would have left about 50,000 tons of free paper, if their machines continued to produce at the same rate as in 1916. In addition to this quantity there was some free paper available from Canadian mills. On this basis there would have been at least 100,000 tons of free paper available for the whole year. But subsequent information indicates that because of car shortage and other abnormal conditions the news-print mills will not be able to equal their 1916 record, so that the surplus of free paper will probably be somewhat less than 100,000 tons.

The contract and moral obligations reported by domestic manufacturers, however, included a considerable quantity of paper that was to be supplied to jobbers, and it is safe to assume that a considerable portion of this is free tonnage and would be available to those publishers who are dependent upon the open market. These facts with respect to the commitments and free tonnage of manufacturers and the requirements of publishers support the conclusion that the supply during 1917 will probably be sufficient to meet the minimum requirements of consumers, if they economize in every way possible. The balance between consumption and production, however, is very close, and present abnormal conditions are constantly putting added pressure upon publishers to increase their circulation, so that there is little prospect of a substantial improvement in market conditions during the continuance of the war.

Section 6. Conclusions.

The facts stated on the preceding pages indicate that there was a scarcity of news print paper in 1916. A small increase in domestic production is shown; but there was a large increase in demand, both domestic and foreign, and imports were not sufficient to meet this increase. As a result stocks were materially reduced.

This scarcity, however, was undoubtedly exaggerated by articles published in trade papers and by the emphasis given it by the manufacturers through their association and by the jobbers. This resulted in an abnormal multiplication of orders caused by panic conditions thus partly brought about. The result was a bidding up of prices, giving the appearance of a much greater demand than actually existed.

All the data in the Commission's possession indicate that there will probably be enough paper to meet the minimum needs during 1917, if publishers will practice economy in every way possible. The effect of the war conditions now existing will probably be to stimulate demand and reduce the supply.

CHAPTER VII.

EVIDENCE OF VIOLATIONS OF THE ANTITRUST LAWS.

Section 1. The News-Print Manufacturers Association.

Substantial evidence is in the possession of the Commission tending to show violations of the Federal antitrust laws by certain manufacturers of news-print paper who are members of the voluntary association known as the News Print Manufacturers Association, with headquarters at 18 East Forty-first Street, New York City. Its membership includes practically all of the Canadian manufacturers as well as all the United States producers except one large and a few smaller ones. About 86 per cent of the effective production[1] of news-print paper of the North American Continent is included in the association. The five members of the executive committee of the association, who, with the secretary, manage its affairs, speak directly for more than one-third of the total news-print tonnage of the continent. Mr. George F. Steele, of New York, the secretary of the association, is its admitted active central agent.[2]

The organization has no articles of association and no by-laws. Its expenses are defrayed by assessments of members on the basis of tonnage output. Neither it nor its executive committee keeps any written minutes or records. Meetings of the executive committee and of the association are held at the call of the secretary, and usually in turn at New York, Montreal, and Chicago. Policies are decided upon at the various meetings or through correspondence between the secretary and different members. As a rule they are put into effect on notification by the secretary. The secretary, by frequent use of the telephone, also keeps in close touch with each of the members of the executive committee, as well as with certain distributing agencies and other persons prominent in the industry.

Ostensibly the association is organized for the collection and dissemination of statistics. Actually, however, its principal energies have been diverted to other activities. The evidence in the hands of the Commission (consisting largely of correspondence between the active parties and of interviews) tends to show that the acts

---

[1] Effective production refers to that part of news-print paper in the market for publishers. It does not include some news print controlled by publishers and some which is used in the production of wall paper. In 1916, 82 per cent of the total production on the North American Continent was produced by members of the association.

[2] For further details in regard to the association, see Chap. II, sec. 5.

of the association officers and members have transcended innocent purposes and resulted in substantial suppression of competition and restraint of trade.

Section 2. Allotment of customers.

Competition in the selling of news-print paper in both the United States and Canada has been prevented by the allotment of customers or by the noninterference by association members with the customers of any other member.

These efforts to control constitute one factor in the present situation. Writing to a manufacturer under date of March 17, 1916, the secretary of the association says (after referring to the disparity of costs between what he calls the larger and smaller mills, which latter are compelled to purchase their sulphite):

> If the prices were put up to a point sufficient to protect them, the profits made by these larger concerns would be simply astounding. On the other hand, what are the smaller mills going to do if the price of paper does not go up?
>
> *   *   *   *   *   *   *
>
> There seems to be only one way out of the difficulty for them, and that is for the larger mills to take the contracts and those smaller mills to depend on current business until the war is over and then bring about a readjustment of contracts. There is good reason why this current business should pay a high price, and it seems to me that it should be turned over to the mills who do not supply their own raw material and will have to pay well for their chemical pulp.
>
> *   *   *   *   *   *   *
>
> This is a matter which will be discussed fully at the meeting next Thursday and Friday in Montreal, and I am going to try to bring about an arrangement of that sort for the production of the smaller concerns.

It was elicited at the recent hearings before the Commission that such allotment of customers and business exists in the present organization of the trade.

As a result, and as the evidence shows, except where news-print mills have ceased to make news-print paper and have thus left their customers in the open market, or where occasionally a mill not in the association has made a lower price to obtain a needed customer—there have been very few instances of competition in selling in the news-print paper industry. In fact, so few are these cases that each is known and referred to by name in the trade. Such instances of competition of any size as did occur were either arbitrated or apologized for and promises of nonrepetition demanded and made.

The effect of these practices appears to be the undue enhancement of prices to small publishers and a widening of the disparity in prices charged the customers of different mills.

Section 3. Prorating and absorbing tonnage of new mills.

By the surrender pro rata of customers to absorb the tonnage of new mills as it comes on the market, such new competitors have been prevented from selling any paper in open competition.

The power of the association entirely to suppress the threatened competition of new mills has been exercised in at least three instances. The Price Bros.' mill and the Abitibi mill, of Canada, are both large, new, and efficient mills and therefore potentially powerful competitors. The customers required by them, in order to keep their production off the competitive market, were surrendered to them pro rata by members of the association, so that substantially no tonnage therefrom came into the market as competitive. Successful efforts were made to prevent competition from the tonnage of the Union Bag & Paper Co.'s new news print mill at Three Rivers, Quebec. Its tonnage is to be sold through the Canadian Export Paper Co. (See p. 42.)

It is apparent that there is no necessity for any price agreement under any scheme of allotment either of customers or of territory among the various producing units when such division of business is respected. Each producer is then at liberty to charge his customers whatever the traffic will bear without the restraining influence of competition. Particularly are such schemes effective when, as in the present situation, all over-seas importation of paper is cut off.

Section 4. Curtailment of production.

In 1915 the association attempted the curtailment of the production of those engaged in the manufacture of news-print paper. It has also endeavored to prevent existing producers from increasing their facilities for production.

On the latter point, although the secretary, at a meeting in Montreal in October, 1915, stated that—

> We were on the verge of a revival of business such as has rarely before been experienced in this country.

and that—

> I stated to those who were assembled at the Montreal meeting that it appeared to me as if prosperity was knocking at our door,

yet, notwithstanding such knowledge or prediction, efforts were continued throughout that month to prevent one company from putting in a new machine for the manufacture of news print, even to the extent of attempting to buy certain water power, "so as to stall his plans of putting a paper mill in there"—this is the language of the person who made the attempt.

Section 5. Canadian joint selling agency.

On August 15, 1916, a charter was granted to the Canadian Export Paper Co., of Montreal, with an authorized capital stock of $500,000. The form of contract for subscription to stock in that company shows that each paper-manufacturing company, by subscribing thereto, agrees to place in the hands of the Canadian Export Paper Co. the sale of all of its news-print paper tonnage (except that sold in Canada) and that the proceeds of such sales should be prorated among the constituent concerns.

Five Canadian concerns—The Laurentide Co., Price Bros., Belgo-Canadian, Donnacona, and Brompton Pulp & Paper Co.—are members of this export company. It is expected that other Canadian mills will become members or put their tonnage at its disposal, and the export company will sell "as though it were the product of one concern" the total export tonnage of its constituent members or principals, all of whom are normal competitors, and whose aggregate output comprises more than one-third of all the news-print paper produced in Canada. In 1915 about 75 per cent and in 1916 about 77 per cent of the total Canadian output was imported into the United States. (See Chap. II, sec. 7.)

The sales agents of the Export Paper Co. have already been active in the United States. Through this joint agency that competition, if any, which previously may have existed or which might now normally exist between the member concerns in bidding for trade in the United States has been entirely suppressed.

It should be stated in this connection that the correspondence shows that the secretary of the association urged the formation of this company and that the constituent companies are also members of the News Print Manufacturers Association, and that the Laurentide company is represented on the executive committee of the association. The possible results of the control of one-third of the total Canadian tonnage through the executive committee of the News Print Manufacturers Association in diverting such supplies from the United States and artificially starving the domestic market can easily be appreciated.

Section 6. Other activities.

Substantial evidence of other activities tending to restraint of trade or in aid or furtherance of such restraint is also in the hands of the Commission. This evidence may be summarized as follows:

(a) Two campaigns among the news-print manufacturers were prosecuted through the secretary of the News Print Manufacturers Association, urging that such manufacturers take steps to show general and large increases in costs as a justification for proposed sharp advance in prices. The first campaign, in the winter of 1915–16, apparently failed to make the desired showing. A number of mills answered that there had been no particular increase in costs or that if slight increases had occurred they had been offset by certain savings. The second campaign occurred in May and June, 1916. It was then emphatically impressed upon the mills that in their cost statements all materials used should, regardless of actual costs, be figured as though bought in the current open market, when such was not the case.

(*b*) Substantially all paper sold to publishers is sold on the condition that it be used only by the purchaser. This practice results in closer control of the supply of paper and prevents any accumulation of stocks which might be offered in competition with the supply from the mills.

(*c*) Some mills, which buy pulp wood, have made and generally respect a division of territory and do not bid against each other in the purchase of such wood.

(*d*) The business of most of the smaller publishers is now divided among jobbers and distributing agencies. Indications are that in certain States or sections the smaller publishers are unable to obtain quotations except from the specific jobbers to whom their district is apparently assigned. The fact that, as a rule, mills will not quote to these smaller publishers also indicates close relationship between mills and distributing agencies in such division of territory.

CHAPTER VIII.

SUMMARY OF PRINCIPAL FACTS WITH CONCLUSIONS AND RECOMMENDATIONS.

Section 1. Principal facts.

News-print paper is produced in North America by approximately 80 manufacturing plants, of which, in 1916, 63 were located in the United States and 17 in Canada. Approximately 75 per cent of the Canadian production is consumed in the United States.

The costs of producing news-print paper depend upon varying factors, to wit, the size and integration of the plant, its access to supplies of wood, the character and cost of its water power, and the efficiency of equipment and management. The large mills, which generally are the most efficient, usually make contracts for their entire output for a year in advance with the large metropolitan papers for the bulk of their tonnage. Some large contracts have been made for periods of from three to five years. The smaller mills, and those which are operating at higher costs, usually supply the smaller publishers and sell a larger proportion of their output in the open market, through jobbers, at higher prices.

COSTS OF PRODUCTION.—For the first six months of the year 1916 average costs had not increased over the last half of the year preceding. For the next four months, up to October 1, 1916, the average increase of costs in the chief American mills was about $1.50 per ton. By December of 1916 and January of 1917 average costs in these mills had increased $5.52 per ton over the costs of the first six months of 1916, the increase in particular mills ranging from $1 to $19 per ton. It has been estimated that the average advance for the first half of 1917 would be between $5 and $10 per ton. Informal estimates made by the officials of the Canadian Government placed the maximum increase in cost of production at $10 per ton for Canadian mills, and prices were agreed upon with the Canadian Government by which publishers were furnished with news-print paper at the following prices: $2.50 per 100 pounds for rolls and $3.25 for sheets in car lots and $3.50 per 100 pounds for sheets in less-than-car lots. These prices are subject to revision after June 1, 1917.

PRESENT CONDITIONS SERIOUS.—Conditions in the newspaper publishing business were reported by the Commission in March as serious

132

and they continue to be serious. Within the year prices to large consumers of print paper have been advanced from about $40 per ton to over $60 and $70 per ton, and in some cases even up to $90 per ton. Also, by concerted action the terms of contracts have been so changed as to shift a considerable financial burden from the manufacturers to the publishers. To some of the larger newspapers of the country this price increase means, in some instances, an increase in paper cost of hundreds of thousands of dollars. This, in many cases, will not only cause the loss of profits for the year, but a serious financial embarrassment of the publication itself.

The smaller publishers have been forced to pay prices as high as $150 and $180 per ton. In addition to the above increase of prices among publishers of minor dailies and weeklies, it is complained that they found great difficulty in getting paper at any price, and to a large number of such publishers in the country the increase in the price means the difference between a living margin and the complete ruin of their business and the suspension of their publications.

The financial strength of great daily publications may enable them to survive; it is the smaller newspapers that will probably suffer the most seriously if these conditions continue. The small weekly and daily publications of the country particularly serve a great and useful purpose in the dissemination of facts and in the creation of an intelligent public opinion, and such disaster as impends by reason of this increase in the price of news-print paper makes the question one of great public concern.

CAUSES OF EXISTING CONDITIONS.—The existing situation is partly due to conditions of supply and demand. On account of the increase in advertising and news matter, there has been an increase in the demand for news-print paper. The supply of news-print paper available for domestic consumption increased from 1,644,000 tons in 1915 to 1,816,000 tons in 1916, an increase of 172,000 tons for the year 1916 over the year 1915. On January 1, 1916, the stocks of news-print paper carried by manufacturers were about 69,000 tons. At the end of 1916 these stocks were reduced to approximately 42,000 tons. While during 1916 prices advanced to an extraordinarily high level and there were difficulties in procuring paper, it is nevertheless a fact that newspapers were generally able to secure news-print paper for their reasonable requirements if they would pay very high prices. The quantity manufactured during the year was equal, therefore, to that needed for reasonable requirements of newspapers within approximately 27,000 tons, which quantity was taken from the reserve stocks. It is probable that if publishers will exercise the strictest economy the supply will be equal to the requirements for the year 1917.

The close balance between supply and demand inevitably tended to create general uneasiness. There is much evidence that manufacturers, instead of attempting to allay this natural fear on the part of the publishers, played upon it deliberately. A panic market was the result. While there was approximately enough paper to go around, publishers were fearful that they could not get their supply. They tried to place orders with many mills and duplicated the placing of their orders for the purpose of being assured of a supply. Newspapers which had difficulty in closing contracts or which were fearful lest their supply under contract would prove inadequate went into the open market. The result was that requirements were made to appear many times greater than they actually were, and a fictitious demand was thus created, which produced a condition of panic with panic prices.

While these conditions obtained and would naturally have some influence upon price, it is the opinion of the Commission that the prices were actually made in the industry without the operation of free competitive influences in their determination. By means of a trade association, organized ostensibly for a lawful purpose, conditions in the market were substantially influenced in a manner which would not be possible under conditions of free competition. Concert of action was made possible through this association in the matter of discouraging new production of news-print paper, in the allotment of customers, in the promotion of fear that the supply would not be equal to the demand, in disseminating propaganda justifying higher prices because of alleged higher costs, and in other ways. The increase in the prices charged are not justified by the increased costs of production.

Section 2. Conclusions.

From the facts disclosed during the investigation, the Commission submits the following conclusions:

1. The increases in the selling prices of news-print paper for the year 1917 in most cases were greater than could be justified by the increases in cost.

2. There is not now, and has not been, such a serious shortage of news-print paper as to warrant the extremely high prices generally charged. The Commission finds that there is enough news-print paper to meet all the strictly necessary demands of publishers during 1917. There is, however, a close balance between supply and demand, so that the strictest economy in the use of news-print paper is necessary.

3. The system of distribution of news-print paper is faulty. By reason of this fact this close balance between supply and demand could easily be developed into local shortage, and this condition was taken advantage of and exaggerated by artificial means. Reports of

alleged shortage were widely circulated for the purpose of justifying high prices. Keen competition among the comparatively unorganized publishers, who, in their anxiety to assure themselves of their necessary supplies of paper, bid feverishly in the open market, helped to make the situation more acute.

4. The increase in prices has been due in part to the fact that free competition has been seriously restricted in the news-print paper industry. Important manufacturers in the United States and Canada were banded together to secure unreasonable profits.

5. Some small publishers have already been put out of business and more are likely to suffer the same fate, and some large publishers will be financially ruined and many others will be unable to make any profits unless conditions are remedied.

6. While jobbers have been severely criticized in respect to the prices charged by them, the Commission has found many instances in which the mills have compelled the jobbers to pay exceedingly high prices, and in those instances it has been necessary for the jobbers in turn to charge extremely high prices to their customers. In some instances, however, it was found that jobbers who bought paper at reasonably low prices took advantage of their opportunity to sell at unreasonably high prices.

Section 3. Efforts of the Commission to afford relief.

The Commission, while directing its efforts to a discovery of the facts affecting the economic and legal sides of the question, sought also, within the limitations of its power, to restore competitive conditions in the industry and at the same time to bring such immediate practical relief as would prevent serious financial distress and injury to publishers while the processes of competition were being restored. Public hearings were held, at which these several interests appeared, and many conferences were had with them. The efforts of the Commission were made in the public interest, but some of them without express authority of law. Its aim was to act as arbiter in the situation for the purpose of securing prompt relief. It was particularly desired to provide some means whereby the smaller publishers could be relieved with respect to their most pressing necessities. The various interested parties, however, failed to come to any agreement among themselves. But, largely as a result of the Commission's activities, some substantial relief was obtained for smaller publishers in various sections of the country through the cooperation of certain manufacturers, jobbers, and publishers.

PROPOSAL OF MANUFACTURERS.—Following the activities of the Commission, certain manufacturers producing in the aggregate about one-third of the total tonnage of news-print paper in the United

States and Canada submitted the following proposal to the Commission:

Whereas among manufacturers and publishers there are differences of opinion regarding the increase since January, 1916, in the cost of production of news-print paper in the United States, and regarding the increased prices to which manufacturers are entitled for news-print paper sold for use in the United States for the six months' period beginning March 1, 1917, taking into consideration the increase in their cost of production and other conditions affecting such manufacturers; and

Whereas the undersigned manufacturers are desirous of cooperating in any plan that may be approved by the Federal Trade Commission providing for a more effective distribution of news-print paper among the smaller publishers; and

Whereas the undersigned manufacturers are desirous of submitting these matters to the arbitrament of the Federal Trade Commission:

Now, therefore, Each of the undersigned does hereby request the Federal Trade Commission to find, fix, and determine forthwith—

(*a*) The probable or estimated increased cost of production of standard news-print paper in the United States during the period of time commencing March 1, 1917, and ending September 1, 1917, over the cost of production of news-print paper in the United States during the year 1916.

(*b*) What price per hundred pounds at the mill would be a fair and reasonable price for the sale of such paper for use in the United States during the aforesaid period of time from March 1, 1917, to September 1, 1917, taking into consideration such increased cost of production and other conditions affecting respective manufacturers which the Commission may deem pertinent at this time?

And each of the undersigned does hereby agree that it will carry out and complete at the prices and on the terms therein stated all of its existing contracts for the sale of such paper which were made at a price or prices as low as or lower than the price or prices so found, fixed, or determined by said Commission to be fair and reasonable for said period commencing March 1, 1917, and ending September 1, 1917, and that with respect to contracts which are for higher prices than those so found, fixed, and determined by said Commission for said last-mentioned period of time it will supply such contract purchasers with their necessary requirements only of such paper at a price not in excess of the amount so found, fixed, or determined by the Federal Trade Commission to be a fair and reasonable maximum price on such paper, as aforesaid, during said period of time from March 1, 1917, to September 1, 1917.

The purpose of limiting such last-mentioned contract purchasers to an amount of paper which will supply their necessary requirements only is to enable each of the undersigned to supply other, and particularly small, publishers who have no contracts with sufficient paper to cover their necessary requirements from time to time during said period of time; and consequently in the event that any dispute arises at any time between any undersigned manufacturer and such contract purchaser, or that any complaint is made to the Federal Trade Commission at any time concerning the question as to whether or not such contract purchaser is getting more than his necessary requirements only of paper during said period of time, then, and in that event, the Federal Trade Commission shall have the right, and is hereby authorized, to determine in each of said instances the amount of paper which is needed to supply the necessary requirements only of such contract purchaser, and the latter shall not be entitled to receive any reduction from his contract price for any paper during said period unless he has filed with this Commission his written consent to this arbitration and its terms.

And each of the undersigned does hereby agree that it will, so far as lies in its power, limit each contract purchaser to his necessary requirements only and sell to its customers, respectively, who have no contracts sufficient paper to meet their necessary requirements only during said period of time at a price not in excess of the amount found, fixed, and determined by the Federal Trade Commission to be a fair and reasonable maximum price on such paper.

While this arrangement is to run for only six months, it is understood that the contract prices named in contracts with publishers heretofore made which may be reduced by the action of the commission hereinunder are not hereafter to determine the price to be paid for news-print paper by such contract purchasers as consent to this arbitration.

And the undersigned does also agree and bind itself to cooperate with the Federal Trade Commission in carrying out any plan approved by the Commission to bring about the distribution of news-print paper for the purpose of securing prompt and effective relief to the small publishers of the United States and which will enable such small publishers, through cooperative buying, to secure their news-print paper at practically the same price as that which is hereinunder to be enjoyed by the larger publishers, due provision being made for any additional cost of distribution. New publishers shall not be charged more than said maximum price so found, fixed, and determined by the Federal Trade Commission during said period of time.

And each of the undersigned, while not admitting but on the contrary expressly denying that any law has been violated by it, does nevertheless hereby agree that the Federal Trade Commission may, if it finds it necessary or advisable, proceed forthwith to make recommendations for the readjustment of its business in order that it may maintain its organization, management, and conduct of business in accordance with law.

Respectfully yours,

INTERNATIONAL PAPER CO.,
By P. T. DODGE, *President.*
ABITIBI POWER & PAPER CO. (LTD.),
By ALEXANDER SMITH, *Vice President.*
THE SPANISH RIVER PULP & PAPER MILLS (LTD.),
By GEO. H. MEAD, *President.*
THE LAURENTIDE CO. (LTD.),
By GEORGE CHAHOON, Jr., *President.*
THE BELGO-CANADIAN PULP & PAPER CO.,
By W. H. BIERMAN, *General Manager.*
THE NORTHWEST PAPER CO.,
By C. I. McNAIR, *General Manager.*
TAGGARTS PAPER CO.,
By G. C. SHERMAN, *President.*

FEBRUARY 15, 1917.

To the FEDERAL TRADE COMMISSION,
Washington, D. C.

ACTION OF PUBLISHERS.—When the proposal of the manufacturers was made known to newspaper publishers a number of the larger of them agreed that if the price in their contracts made for the purchase of paper should be reduced to the maximum price to be

determined by the Commission for the period of six months from
March 1, 1917, they would release each month up to 5 per cent of
their tonnage under contract, it being understood that such released
paper would be used in the manner to be determined by the Commission to help publishers without contracts.

ACTION OF JOBBERS.—As the needs of the smaller publishers,
widely scattered throughout the country, were most urgent, and
since they were largely dependent upon the paper jobbers for their
supplies, and as such jobbers appeared to be the only means at hand
for supplying these small publishers promptly, the Commission
deemed it advisable to call the jobbers for a conference. The result
was that the leading jobbers entered into an agreement to handle
and distribute such news-print paper as the Commission might place
at their disposal at fair and reasonable maximum rates of compensation as follows:

> Single car lots direct from mill, not to exceed 5 per cent on f. o. b. mill
> price.
> Less than carload lots, but not less than ton lots, delivered from warehouse, not to exceed 12½ per cent on cost in warehouse.
> Less than ton lots, delivered from warehouse, not to exceed 20 per cent on
> cost in warehouse.

The agreement also provided that the jobbers during the period
covered by it would handle all their news-print tonnage sold to
publishers on the above rates of gross profit figured on current replacement value, and also that they would sell for cash or on approved credit in carload lots to the representative of any association
of publishers at the same prices as to individuals.

FINDINGS OF THE COMMISSION AS TO FAIR PRICES.—Two specific phases
of relief were presented in the proposal of the manufacturers set
out above, (1) the matter of price reduction directly effecting the
saving of millions to publishers, and (2) a more equitable distribution of paper supply directly benefiting the smaller publishers, not
only saving them money, but preserving many of them from suspension and bankruptcy.

The second phase, that relating to the distribution of paper to
the smaller publishers, while requiring a relatively small quantity
of paper, was the most difficult of accomplishment. It was hoped
that this paper would be obtained in part by the proposal of the
larger publishers indicated above.

The proposal of the manufacturers and the action of jobbers and
publishers having been defined, the Commission decided to accept the
difficult task of arbiter. In so doing it did not purport to act as an
agency of government to fix prices, but, on the contrary, to serve
only as an arbitrator.

The Commission's findings were as follows:

(1) That a fair and reasonable price for the sale of standard news-print paper in rolls by each of the aforesaid signatory manufacturers for use in the United States during the six months' period of time beginning March 1, 1917, and ending August 31, 1917, is the sum of $2.50 per 100 pounds f. o. b. at the mill in carload lots and is the sum of $2.75 per 100 pounds f. o. b. at the mill in less-than-carload lots.

(2) That a fair and reasonable price for the sale of standard news-print paper in sheets by each of the aforesaid signatory manufacturers for use in the United States during the aforesaid six months' period of time is the sum of $3.25 per 100 pounds f. o. b. at the mill in carload lots and is the sum of $3.50 per 100 pounds f. o. b. at the mill in less-than-carload lots.

(3) That no publisher or jobber who has an existing contract with any of the aforesaid signatory manufacturers for standard news-print paper at a higher price or prices than is hereby found to be fair and reasonable shall be entitled to receive or be given the benefit of such reduced prices unless he files with this Commission prior to March 20, 1917, his written agreement to waive and release for sale and distribution to publishers only, who have no contracts, 5 per cent of the total amount of tonnage specified in such contract.

(4) That if any extraordinary new conditions hereafter arise which make it unjust to the aforesaid signatory manufacturers to continue the aforesaid prices during the full period of said six months, this Commission will readjust the same for the whole or any remaining part of the three months commencing June 1 and ending August 31, 1917; provided that said signatory manufacturers file with this Commission their written request so to do; and provided further that, in the opinion of this Commission, the facts presented in such petition requires such action in order to prevent plain injustice.

In making this award the Commission stated that it was of the opinion that the foregoing prices for news-print paper would not produce a fair and reasonable profit for some of the smaller mills under the unusual conditions now existing as to the cost of ground wood and sulphite. They produce not over 18 per cent of the tonnage of the North American Continent.

Further, it was of the opinion that on the basis of their respective costs of production, the foregoing prices were also fair and reasonable for each and all of the following manufacturers who did not join in this proposal:

Minnesota & Ontario Power Co., including its subsidiary, the Fort Frances Pulp & Paper Co. (Ltd.).
Gould Paper Co.
Finch, Pruyn & Co.
Great Northern Paper Co.
Pejepscot Paper Co.
Crown Willamette Paper Co.
St. Croix Paper Co.
Price Bros. & Co. (Ltd.)
Donnacona Paper Co. (Ltd.)
Powell River Co.

In addition to the above companies, the Consolidated Water Power & Paper Co. and the Wisconsin River Pulp & Paper Co. could sell at a slight advance over the prices named and make a fair profit. It should also be stated that the Great Northern Paper Co., appearing in the above list, is and has been selling most of its output at prices as low or lower than those named; and it should be further stated that the Powell River Co. and the Crown Willamette Paper Co have much tonnage under long-time contracts at lower prices.

As soon as this award was announced a majority of the contract customers of the signatory manufacturers signed the agreement with the Commission to release 5 per cent of their tonnage and to eliminate returns. Some of the customers of the International Paper Co. found it impossible to sign this agreement, because they had already been reduced in their tonnage from 10 to 20 per cent below what they consumed during the preceding year. Other customers of the International Paper Co. refrained from signing the agreement fearing that it would cancel their contracts and leave them in the open market at the end of the period covered by the arbitration. This fear was incited in some instances by the activities of the International's sales agents.

In order to reach a satisfactory settlement of this and other doubtful matters connected with the arbitration, negotiations were continued with the signatory manufacturers during the month of March, 1917. Efforts were also made during this period to induce several other large manufacturers to join in the agreement. Before these matters were disposed of the Commission was notified by the Department of Justice that it intended to continue proceedings against the news-print manufacturers.

On April 11, 1917, the Federal grand jury for the southern district of New York brought indictments against the following news-print manufacturers for violation of the Sherman law:

>Philip T. Dodge, International Paper Co.
>George H. Mead, Spanish River Pulp & Paper Mills (Ltd.).
>Alexander Smith, Abitibi Power & Paper Co.
>George Chahoon, jr., Laurentide Co.
>G. H. P. Gould, Gould and Donnacona Paper Cos.
>E. W. Backus, Minnesota & Ontario Paper Co.
>Frank J. Sensenbrenner, Kimberly-Clark Co.

The first four of the indicted manufacturers were signatories to the arbitration agreement.

Having heard nothing from these manufacturers after the indictments were brought, the Commission on April 21, 1917, sent them a list of their contract customers who had signed up and requested them to state what means they had taken to give these publishers the benefits of the arbitration agreement, and what disposition they were prepared to make of the 5 per cent of contract tonnage of paper surrendered by these publishers.

To this letter the manufacturers replied that in view of the indictments, which were unexpected when the agreement was entered into, they desired to give the matter further consideration. During the last week of May, 1917, counsel for two of the indicted manufacturers notified the Commission that his clients had decided to withdraw from the arbitration submission of February 15, 1916.

Section 4. Recommendation.

The withdrawal of the largest manufacturers from the arbitration arrangement resulted in the failure of the effort of the Commission to bring relief to the situation by voluntary cooperation of the interested parties. It, therefore, has decided to recommend as a war emergency measure that Congress by appropriate legislation provide:

(1) That all mills producing and all agencies distributing print paper and mechanical and chemical pulp in the United States be operated on Government account; that these products be pooled in the hands of a Government agency and equitably distributed at a price based upon the cost of production and distribution, plus a fair profit per ton.

(2) That pursuant thereto some Federal agency be empowered and directed to assume the supervision and control thereof during the pendency of the war.

(3) That, by reason of the fact that approximately 75 per cent of the production of news-print paper in Canada comes into the United States, proper action be taken to secure the cooperation of the Canadian Government in the creation of a similar governmental agency for the same function, which shall be clothed with power and authority to act jointly with the governmental agency of the United States for the protection of the consumers and manufacturers of print paper and the public of the United States and Canada.

(4) That in case the Canadian Government shall not join in such a cooperative enterprise, then importation of paper and mechanical and chemical pulp into the United States shall be made only on Government account to or through the Federal agency charged with such supervision and distribution.

EXHIBITS.

EXHIBIT 1.

PETITION OF THE NEWS PRINT MANUFACTURERS ASSOCIATION TO THE FEDERAL TRADE COMMISSION.

IN THE MATTER OF THE OWEN RESOLUTION RESPECTING PRINT PAPER.

To the Honorable, Federal Trade Commission of the United States of America:

Your petitioner, the Executive Committee of the News Print Manufacturers Association, respectfully represents:

1. That the News Print Manufacturers Association is an organization formed by a number of manufacturers of news-print paper in the United States and Canada for the purpose of promoting the interest of the print paper industry in said countries.

2. That the attention of the undersigned has been called to the fact that a number of resolutions have been introduced into the Congress of the United States urging that an investigation be made by this Commission with a view of determining the reason for the alleged increase to the publishers in the United States of the cost of print paper; and that Mr. Owen submitted the following resolution which was considered and agreed to:

[64th Cong., 1st sess.; S. Res. 177; in the Senate of the United States; Apr. 24, 1916.]

Mr. Owen submitted the following resolution; which was considered and agreed to.

RESOLUTION.

Resolved, That the Trade Commission is hereby requested to inquire into the increase of the price of print paper during the last year and ascertain whether or not the newspapers of the United States are being subjected to unfair practices in the sale of print paper.

3. That the undersigned manufacturers of print paper who manufacture approximately fifty (50%) per cent of the total tonnage of print paper used in the United States, respectfully represents to your Honorable Commission:

(a) That about eighty-five per cent of the news-print paper manufactured in the United States and Canada is sold on annual contracts and these contract prices have not increased more than one per cent during the past twelve months, and will not average any higher than the price at which it was contracted and sold during the past ten years, whereas the price of book and wrapping paper have increased approximately one hundred per cent.

(b) That because of adverse newspaper comment in news items and interviews in the public press the undersigned as manufacturers of print paper have been grossly misrepresented.

And respectfully request your Honorable Commission that as soon as it can be done an investigation be had by your body into this question in accordance

142

with the Senate resolution above set forth; and these petitioners respectfully state that they will consider it a privilege to furnish this Commission any information within their power.

Respectfully submitted.

> NEWS PRINT MANUFACTURERS ASSOCIATION,
> PHILIP C. DODGE,
> GEORGE H. MEAD,
> J. H. A. ACER,
> E. W. BACKUS,
> G. H. P. GOULD,
> *Executive Committee.*
> By TIMOTHY T. ANSBERRY,
> *Counsel.*

EXHIBIT 2.

THE FEDERAL TRADE COMMISSION'S SUGGESTION OF SMALLER SUNDAY PAPERS.

The letter below was sent to all Sunday newspapers in the United States:

OCTOBER 14, 1916.

DEAR SIR: In connection with its investigation of news print prices, the Commission has given serious consideration to possible means of preventing the suspension of papers because of the increasing scarcity and advancing prices. The present situation can only be alleviated by increasing the output or reducing consumption. The Commission has conferred with a number of prominent publishers regarding ways to reduce consumption in addition to the cutting off of returns, eliminating wastes, etc., which many newspapers are reported to have already done. These publishers are of the opinion that there is still an opportunity to effect a considerable reduction in consumption by cutting down the size of Sunday papers. They feel that the elimination of certain features would meet with public approval and would not decrease the revenues of the publishers. The paper saved by cutting down the size of one large Sunday edition several pages would be sufficient to keep a number of smaller papers supplied for a considerable time. Unless present supplies of paper can be increased, which does not now seem probable, such unselfish action on the part of the large city papers appears to be the only means that will save many of the smaller publishers from going out of business.

The Commission asks your cooperation in this matter and would like to know your attitude toward this proposition. The Commission would also appreciate any suggestions that occur to you regarding practical ways of making this proposal effective.

A franked envelope, which requires no postage, is enclosed for your reply.

Very truly yours,

> EDWARD N. HURLEY,
> *Chairman.*

Answers to this letter were received from more than 100 publishers. The purport of these answers has been summarized below. In order to measure their significance more accurately they have been classified according to circulation.

The Chicago Tribune, whose Sunday edition has a circulation of over 600,000, had noticed a detriment to its business from a cut of four pages in the Sunday color section, and did "not feel warranted in making a further cut in the Sunday paper."

The Boston Post, which has a circulation of over 450,000, answered, in part, as follows:

> We have also materially reduced the size of our issues, using two pages less several days per week than we would use if there were an unlimited supply of news print. We are prepared to go even further than this in cooperation with other papers, and would willingly omit one edition each week. That is a move, however, so radical that it could not be accomplished without a general agreement.

A publishing company in the Middle West, whose dailies in different cities have a combined circulation of over 200,000, reported lack of success in an attempt to obtain the cooperation of other publishers in putting the proposals of the Commission into practice. The hope was expressed that the Commission might be able to bring about cooperation under a signed agreement.

Replies were received from nine papers, each with a circulation of more than 100,000 but less than 200,000. Six of these announced that they were already acting in accordance with the proposals of the Commission. A Pittsburgh paper said "in Pittsburgh the publishers have already considered and taken steps to lessen the consumption of paper in the Sunday editions," and recommended that the Commission "bring the various publishers in their respective cities into consultation." This plan was also advocated by a Minneapolis managing editor as follows:

> To me the most practical means to this end seems to lie in personal efforts of the members of the Federal Trade Commission in bringing about agreements in any one locality to an approximately uniform cut in the Sunday issues. I believe that if you were to meet personally the managers of newspapers in each of the large cities you could effect a decided cut in almost all cases.

A St. Louis paper in this group reported that in July, August and September it had reduced its consumption an average of four tons a day below that of June, 1916.[a] Another of this group wrote as follows:

> We are in receipt of your communication in which you recommend that large Sunday newspapers cut down the size of their publication by eliminating several pages of uninteresting features.
> You were right in surmising that such a move would meet with the public approval for the reason that we have made a success of a Sunday newspaper that carries no feature supplements whatsoever outside of the usual comic supplement for the little folks.
> The Sunday Journal averages from twenty-eight to thirty-two pages and sells for two cents. In five years' time we have built up a circulation which is practically double that of one of our five cent competitors whose publication is one of the old style Sunday newspapers and fully five times that of one of the other old line Sunday newspapers.

The publisher of a New York paper which had made "sharp" reductions thinks that it "is bound to hurt Sunday papers very much" but that "the details of the situation are imperative." He expressed his desire "to cooperate further" in "common action by all the Sunday newspapers" or by all of "this particular community." A Baltimore paper said: "We do not know how it will be possible for us to carry our revision any further." A Detroit paper in this group which had made considerable reductions in its Sunday editions asked:

> Why, at the same time, should not the publishers of the big afternoon newspapers * * * be asked to bear their just share of this retrenchment by reducing the number of editions daily to a necessary minimum. * * * It is a problem * * * which * * * will require a concerted effort and the unanimous cooperation of all the newspapers of the country.

---

[a] It is not improbable that its consumption in June was abnormally heavy on account of the political conventions in that month.

Of papers having a circulation of over 50,000 but under 75,000, seven made replies. Six of these reported that they had already put the recommendations into practice. One publisher argued for the large newspaper where quantity is not obtained at the expense of quality, "in order," as he writes, "to do my proper part in counteracting any impression you may have that ordinary newspapers, as commonly operated at present, can be improved by drastic cuts in their size." He quoted the experience of his own paper, however, to show "that mere bulk is not essential to success in daily journalism." The publisher of a Seattle paper in this group wrote:

> I recently made a canvass of the papers of Portland, Oregon, of San Francisco, and of Los Angeles, California, and could not find a case where any newspaper in either of those three cities had made the slightest effort toward economy in the use of white paper.

A Pittsburgh editor wrote "if other cities were making the same efforts in the way of economies that Pittsburgers are, it would, I believe, do much to solve the paper situation." A Minnesota publishing company wrote as follows:

> We have been making drastic cuts in the use of white paper since last July. We are prepared to go to any extent in this direction that safety and common sense and cooperation on the part of our competitors in St. Paul, and Minneapolis will permit.

A Mississippi Valley publishing company has been so successful in asking higher prices for its newspapers than are customary that its contribution is given below almost in full:

> The American publishers have violated all of the fundamental rules of business. The whole business is characterized by waste and lack of system. There is more waste and more incompetence in the management of American newspapers than in any other thing in the United States except in one of the large telegraph companies. There is a provincialism among publishers that is distressing. Newspaper publishers are crazy about circulation. In their greed for circulation they put on expenses without regard to where the money is coming from. They hold the price of their paper down and resort to all sorts of schemes to increase advertising. In years past they have used their increased circulation as a club for higher rates. Now the rates have got to a point where the advertiser cannot afford to pay more. The added circulation gives him no more value, and the publisher now is at the end of his rope. The big fellows are calling out to the little ones to save their white paper.
>
> This paper has never sold its white paper at less than cost. We have always made a profit out of our circulation. The immediate solution of this difficulty, and a permanent one, will be to raise the price of newspapers in this country from one to two cents. We get 15 cents a week for our paper. It is retailed to the newsboys, to news companies, to hotels, etc. for 2½ cents. Ours is, then, what we call a five cent paper. And yet charging this money we have the largest circulation of any morning or evening newspaper in the south. We have the circulation because with our margin of profit on white paper, and with our profit from advertising, we are enabled to buy news of quality and quantity that makes the paper worth the money. Those one-cent papers in New York are wholesaled at from 50 to 60 cents a hundred. This amount does not pay for the weight of the white paper. The New York and Chicago publishers have been suggesting everything except the one thing necessary. Let them begin to economize themselves before sending out exhortations to smaller publishers to economize. If they were to raise the price of the New York papers to two cents, the waste circulation would immediately be saved; the total number of papers printed would be reduced, but about the same publicity would be secured and the value to the advertiser would be about the same. Whenever the publishers sell their white paper for what it costs or a little more than it costs, this paper shortage will end.

For 20 years publishers have thrown the burden of the cost of publication upon advertising, and having to crowd in so much advertising, and having to do so many things to get it they, by the very bulk and weight of the business, have weakened their force as an advertising medium.

The one cent newspapers take a lot of cheap advertising, and I might say fraudulent copy, which otherwise they would not do if the circulation income bore a proper proportion of the total expenses. This paper has a larger circulation than any morning or evening newspaper in the south. Our paper is sold to the reader for 15 cents a week; transient reader pays 5¢ a copy. We get from our agents from 8 to 10¢ a week. We get about 12½ cents a week net from our mail subscribers. We sell the paper to news boys in the city for 2½ cents a copy. If our paper was selling for 10¢ a week to the reader and one cent a copy to transients, we would not have more circulation. Everybody in our territory who reads at all takes the paper. The small profit that we make out of the white paper, enables us to print a big paper and to buy an enormous amount of news. The news keeps up the circulation. The subscriber does not quarrel at the price, he gets value received.

Last month our white paper bill was $18,000. Our circulation receipts were around $26,000. If the publishers will make up their minds to sell their paper at a profit, or at cost, matters will quickly be adjusted.

The Washington Star, whose letter was sent out to members by the American Newspaper Publishers Association, wrote as follows:

We are in receipt of your letter of October 14th addressed to the Editor of The Star in regard to the news-print paper situation. You ask for our cooperation, which we are glad to give, in regard to reducing the consumption of paper.

You may be interested in the comparative figures for the month of September 1915 and 1916:

	September.	
	1915	1916
Amount of paper actually used........................tons..	416	406
Total volume of advertising.......................columns..	2,836	3,078
Volume of reading matter (daily).........................do....	1,950	1,629
Volume of reading matter (Sunday).......................do....	1,027	756
Volume of reading matter (total)..........................do....	2,977	2,385
Total circulation (daily).............................copies..	1,887,923	1,850,467
Returns and adjustments (daily).........................do....	31,907	5,139
Total circulation (Sunday)..............................do....	220,524	227,637
Returns and adjustments (Sunday).......................do....	2,719	966

In the Sunday issue we have greatly reduced the amount of reading matter, eliminating entirely many features and reducing the space occupied by many others. Besides this, in both the daily and Sunday issues, we have, by reducing the news heads and careful editing of news stories, reduced the amount of space now being used for reading matter nearly 20%.

From the circulation we have cut off all returns, and eliminated waste in every way possible. We have constantly been studying every practical means of reducing the consumption and economizing space, but up to this time have not limited the advertising nor cut the reading matter to a point where we feel that we have injured the value of the paper to the reader.

If the news print situation is actually as it has been stated and the consumption continues to exceed the production, there is one of two things left for the publisher to do to reduce the consumption. One is to increase the price at which the paper is sold to the public or the alternative, to increase the rate which is charged the advertiser to a point where the advertising volume will be reduced.

Nineteen papers having circulations of over 25,000 and under 50,000 answered the commission's letter. Sixteen of these had reduced or were trying to reduce their consumption of news-print paper. One of this group, after reciting its very effective economies, says:

> I am of the opinion that the reason more publishers have not put into effect a system to eliminate all waste and to economize on news print is because very few have felt the scarcity, or been affected by the advance in price.

Another says, however, that though fully protected by contract till December 31, 1917, it has cut down its consumption heavily and would be willing to cut the Sunday paper still further if competitors would do likewise, but—"I know * * * at least one of our competitors will not agree to this." Another says that the proper way to get at this is an absolute agreement by all the newspapers. Another urges selling price commensurate with paper cost and prohibition of mailing Sunday papers on Friday night. One publisher writes as follows:

> The fact that a number of the larger newspapers own or control the paper mills that supply them, and will not cooperate, makes it very difficult for other newspapers to economize as they would like to.

Of 30 papers having circulation of over 10,000 and under 25,000, there were 24 that had reduced, or were about to reduce their size. One publisher thought that the remedy lay in refusal of second-class mail privileges under certain conditions. Attention was called by another to the fact that many publishers "are getting their news-print supply under contracts that allow them to do as they choose." One said: "Large Sunday circulations are confined wholly to the metropolitan papers, and it is to them that we must look for large savings of stock." The same point is made by six others. Of these one wrote as follows:

> The publisher, who has been more than forty years in the newspaper business, believes that a very great part of the shortage in news print at the present time is due to extravagance in use, especially by the huge metropolitan Sunday newspapers, who have piled feature upon feature until the bulk of their issues have gone beyond all reason and beyond the actual demand of the reading public; in fact, he has been long convinced that the people would welcome smaller newspapers generally. The only suggestion that I can offer regarding practical ways of making your proposal effective, is to bear strongly in your urgings upon the large newspapers in the great cities. Unless they show disposition toward some unselfish action, there can be no question that the smaller newspapers of the country will be compelled to carry the burden of this abnormal situation.

The publisher of a Baltimore paper expressed his view on the same subject as follows:

> Take Baltimore English language papers as an example. There are two morning papers, three afternoon papers. These 5 daily papers put out every day from 14 to 30 pages each. There are three Sunday papers, putting out from 32 to 70 or more pages each. If these publications would cut down but two pages daily per paper the saving, based on given circulation would amount to the sum of over 32 tons per week—enough to run a dozen small papers.

Another publisher who made the same point prefaced it with an interesting account of his own economies as follows:

> We have furthermore reduced our magazine section, first from 12 pages to 10 and now to 8 pages. The interesting part about this reduction on our part is that we have been able to effect it without materially injuring the standard or quality of our paper and without sacrificing any of our essentially valuable features. We have accomplished it by closer and more discriminating editorship, with the definite purpose in view of making one

word count for two and moderating the typographical display of all matter.
We are very much pleased with the results of our efforts thus far and
feel confident that they can be carried still further.

However, we want to say to you frankly that unless the publishers of
the larger newspapers can be made to see the wisdom of this policy and
put it into effect, the general result is not going to be sufficient to relieve
the situation. The big publishers, with keen and enterprising competition
to meet, hesitate to take the initiative, and any movement in the desired
direction is left to the smaller newspapers in more or less noncompetitive
cities. The decrease in tonnage, therefore, is relatively small when compared to the total, because as you know five or six of the larger cities will
use a greater tonnage than practically all of the smaller cities combined.

A Michigan paper stated that the publishers of that State had already met
to work out plans to economize paper.

Only 19 papers having circulations of over 5,000 and under 10,000 responded
to the Commission's letter. Of these 16 were already trying to reduce their
consumption. One business manager in this group made the point that if the
metropolitan papers would cut down their size, the smaller papers would at
once follow their example. He also suggested the suspension of all papers for
one day.

Of the 21 papers having circulations under 5,000 which replied, 13 were
using less paper than formerly. Several of these papers urged the great importance of economies by the metropolitan dailies.

EXHIBIT 3.

TARIFF DUTIES ON PRINTING PAPER.

Act of March 3, 1883, Schedule M:

Printing paper, unsized, used for books and newspapers exclusively, 15
per cent ad valorem; sized or glued, 20 per cent ad valorem.

Act of October 1, 1890 (McKinley Law), Schedule M, paragraphs 417 to 418:

Printing paper unsized, suitable only for books and newspapers, 15 per
cent ad valorem. Printing paper sized or glued, suitable only for books
and newspapers, 20 per cent ad valorem.

Act of August 27, 1894 (Wilson-Gorman Law), Schedule M, paragraph 306:

Printing paper, unsized, sized or glued, suitable only for books and newspapers, 15 per cent ad valorem.

Act of July 24, 1897 (Dingley Law), Schedule M, paragraph 396:

Printing paper, unsized, sized or glued, suitable for books and newspapers, valued at not above 2 cents per pound, three-tenths of one cent per
pound; valued above 2 cents and not above 2½ cents per pound, four-tenths
of one cent per pound; valued above 2½ cents per pound and not above 3
cents per pound, five-tenths of one cent per pound; valued above 3 cents
and not above 4 cents per pound, six-tenths of one cent per pound; valued
above 4 cents and not above 5 cents per pound, eight-tenths of one cent per
pound; valued above 5 cents per pound, 15 per centum ad valorem:
Provided, That if any country or dependency shall impose an export duty
upon pulp wood exported to the United States, there shall be imposed
upon printing paper when imported from such country or dependency,
an additional duty of one-tenth of one cent per pound for each dollar of
export duty per cord so imposed, and proportionately for fractions of a
dollar of such export duty.

Act of August 5, 1909 (Payne-Aldrich Law), Schedule M, paragraph 409:

Printing paper * * *, unsized, sized, or glued, suitable for the printing of books and newspapers, but not for covers or bindings, not specially
provided for in this section, valued at not above two and one-fourth cents

per pound, three-sixteenths of one cent per pound; valued above two and one-fourth cents and not above two and one-half cents per pound, three-tenths of one cent per pound; valued above two and one-half cents per pound and not above four cents per pound, five-tenths of one cent per pound; valued above four cents and not above five cents per pound, eight-tenths of one cent per pound; valued above five cents per pound, fifteen per centum ad valorem: *Provided, however,* That if any country, dependency, province, or other subdivision of government shall forbid or restrict in any way the exportation of (whether by law, order, regulation, contractural relation, or otherwise, directly or indirectly) or impose any export duty, export license fee, or other export charge of any kind whatsoever * * * upon printing paper, wood pulp, or wood for use in the manufacture of wood pulp, there shall be imposed upon printing paper when imported either directly or indirectly from such country, dependency, province, or other subdivision of government, an additional duty of one-tenth of one cent per pound when valued at three cents per pound, or less, and in addition thereto the amount of such export duty or other export charge imposed by such country, dependency, province, or other subdivision of government, upon printing paper, wood pulp, or wood for use in the manufacture of wood pulp.

Act of July 26, 1911 (Canadian Reciprocity Act), Section 2:

Pulp of wood mechanically ground; pulp of wood, chemical bleached, or unbleached; news print paper, and other paper, and paper board, manufactured from mechanical wood pulp, or from chemical wood pulp, or of which such pulp is the component material of chief value, colored in the pulp, or not colored, and valued at not more than 4 cents per pound, not including printed or decorated wall paper, being the products of Canada, when imported therefrom directly into the United States, shall be admitted free of duty, on the condition precedent that no export duty, export license fee, or other export charge of any kind whatsoever (whether in the form of additional charge or license fee or otherwise), or any prohibition or restriction in any way of the exportation (whether by law, order, regulation, contractual relation, or otherwise, directly or indirectly), shall have been imposed upon such paper, board, or wood pulp, or the wood used in the manufacture of such paper, board, or wood pulp, or the wood pulp used in the manufacture of such paper or board.

Act of October 3, 1913 (Underwood Law), Schedule M, paragraph 322:

Printing paper (other than paper commercially known as handmade or machine handmade paper, japan paper, and imitation japan paper by whatever name known), unsized, sized, or glued, suitable for the printing of books and newspapers, but not for covers or bindings, not specially provided for in this section, valued above 2½ cents per pound, 12 per centum ad valorem: *Provided, however,* That if any country, dependency, province, or other subdivision of government shall impose any export duty, export license fee, or other charge of any kind whatsoever (whether in the form of additional charge or license fee or otherwise) upon printing paper, wood pulp, or wood for use in the manufacture of wood pulp, there shall be imposed upon printing paper, valued above 2½ cents per pound, when imported either directly or indirectly from such country, dependency, province, or other subdivision of government, an additional duty equal to the amount of the highest export duty or other export charge imposed by such country, dependency, province, or other subdivision of government, upon either printing paper, or upon an amount of wood pulp, or wood for use in the manufacture of wood pulp necessary to manufacture such printing paper.

Free List, paragraph 567:

Printing paper (other than paper commercially known as handmade or machine handmade paper, japan paper, and imitation japan paper by whatever name known), unsized, sized, or glued, suitable for the printing of books and newspapers, but not for covers or bindings, not specially provided for in this section, valued at not above 2½ cents per pound, decalcomania paper not printed.

Act of September 8, 1916, section 600, paragraph 322:

Printing paper (other than paper commercially known as hand made or machine hand made paper, japan paper, and imitation japan paper by whatever name known), unsized, sized, or glued, suitable for the printing of books and newspapers, but not for covers or bindings, not specially provided for in this section, valued above 5 cents per pound, twelve per centum ad valorem: *Provided, however,* That if any country, dependency, province, or other subdivision of government shall impose any export duty, export license fee, or other charge of any kind whatsoever (whether in the form of additional charge or license fee or otherwise) upon printing paper, wood pulp, or wood for use in the manufacture of wood pulp, there shall be imposed upon printing paper, valued above 5 cents per pound, when imported directly or indirectly from such country, dependency, province, or other subdivision of government, an additional duty equal to the amount of the highest export duty or other export charge imposed by such country, dependency, province, or other subdivision of government, upon either printing paper or upon an amount of wood pulp, or wood for use in the manufacture of wood pulp necessary to manufacture such printing paper.

Free List, paragraph 567:

Printing paper (other than paper commercially known as hand made or machine hand made paper, japan paper, and imitation japan paper by whatever name known), unsized, sized, or glued, suitable for the printing of books and newspapers, but not for covers or bindings, not specially provided for in this section, valued at not above 5 cents per pound, decalcomania paper not printed.

EXHIBIT 4.

TARIFF DUTIES ON WOOD PULP.

Act of 1883, Schedule M:

A duty of 10 per cent ad valorem was provided upon pulp, dried, for paper makers' use.

Act of 1890, Schedule M, paragraph 415:

Mechanically ground wood pulp, $2.50 per ton, dry weight; chemical wood pulp unbleached, $6.00 per ton, dry weight; bleached, $7.00 per ton, dry weight.

Act of 1894, Schedule M, paragraph 303:

Mechanically ground wood pulp and chemical wood pulp unbleached or bleached, dutiable at the rate of 10 per cent ad valorem.

Act of 1897 (Dingley Law), Schedule M, paragraph 393:

Mechanically ground wood pulp, one-twelfth of one cent per pound, dry weight; chemical wood pulp, unbleached, one-sixth of one cent per pound, dry weight; bleached, one-fourth of one cent per pound, dry weight: *Provided,* That if any country or dependency shall impose an export duty on pulp wood exported to the United States, the amount of such duty shall be added, as an additional duty, to the duties herein imposed upon wood pulp, when imported from such country or dependency.

Act of 1909 (Payne Law); Schedule M, paragraph 406:

Mechanically ground wood pulp, one-twelfth of one cent per pound, dry weight: *Provided, however,* That mechanically ground wood pulp shall be admitted free of duty from any country, dependency, province, or other subdivision of government (being the product thereof) which does not forbid or restrict in any way the exportation of (whether by law, order, regulation, contractual relation, or otherwise, directly or indirectly) or impose any export duty, export license fee, or other export charge of any kind whatsoever, either directly or indirectly (whether in the form of additional charge or license fee or otherwise) upon printing paper, mechanically ground wood pulp, or wood for use in the manufacture of wood pulp: *Provided further,* That if any country, dependency, province, or other subdivision of government, shall impose an export duty or other export charge of any kind whatsoever, either directly or indirectly * * * upon printing paper, mechanically ground wood pulp, or wood for use in the manufacture of wood pulp, the amount of such export duty or other export charge shall be added as an additinal duty to the duty herein imposed upon mechanically ground wood pulp when imported directly or indirectly from such country, dependency, province, or other subdivision of Government. Chemical wood pulp, unbleached, one-sixth of one cent per pound, dry weight; bleached, one-fourth of one cent per pound, dry weight: *Provided,* That if any country, dependency, province, or other subdivision of government shall impose an export duty, or other export charge of any kind whatsoever, either directly or indirectly * * * upon printing paper, chemical wood pulp, or wood for use in the manufacture of wood pulp, the amount of such export duty, or other export charge, shall be added as an additional duty to the duties herein imposed upon chemical wood pulp when imported directly or indirectly from such country, dependency, province, or other subdivision of government.

For provisions of the Canadian reciprocity act of 1911 as to wood pulp, see Exhibit 3.

Act of October 2, 1913 (Underwood Law); free list, paragraph 649:

Mechanically ground wood pulp, chemical wood pulp, unbleached or bleached, and rag pulp.

Exhibit 5.

CONTRACT FORMS FOR THE SALE OF NEWS PRINT.

SPECIFICATIONS OF QUANTITY.

There have heretofore been three common forms of quantity specifications, which were substantially as follows:

Maximum and minimum provision.—That the vendor agrees to sell and deliver, and the vendee agrees to purchase and receive from the vendor, all the news-print paper required in printing and publishing all the editions of the ———, a newspaper published in the city of ———, not exceeding — tons, nor less than — tons.

Leeway provision.—The vendor agrees to sell and furnish to the vendee, and the vendee hereby agrees to purchase and take from the vendor, for use in the publication of the ———, a newspaper published in the city of ———, — tons of news print per year, with a leeway of 5 per cent over or under in quantity.

Entire supply provision.—The vendor agrees to sell and furnish to the vendee, and the vendee hereby agrees to purchase and take from the vendor, for use in the publication of the ———, a newspaper published in the city of ———, their entire supply, *estimated at — tons,* during the period from ——— to ———.

The inadequacy of provisions like those above has been repeatedly demonstrated; under them both the manufacturer and publisher are left in uncertainty.

If publisher desires the maximum quantity or an amount substantially in excess of the approximately estimated tonnage, the manufacturer may have difficulty in meeting his obligations.

If the publisher desires the minimum tonnage, the manufacturer must offer any excess he has provided to meet the contingency, at a reduced price and thus demoralize the open market.

If many publishers simultaneously require the maximum tonnage, the quantity available for purchase in open market is reduced, and publishers not protected by contracts bear the consequences.

The new standard contract seeks to avoid these difficulties by having the tonnage specifically stated, which the manufacturer shall be obliged to deliver, and the publisher to accept and pay for, to be ordered and delivered in definite and equal periodic installments.

Gross weight basis.—Payment according to actual weight of roll as delivered in press room with allowance for weight of core.

Production basis.—Not payment according to pound or ton as above, but upon basis of so many pounds making a thousand 8-page sheets, e. g., 114 pounds per thousand 8-page sheets.

The gross weight basis has been the one in general use, with a standard basis of weight of 32 pounds per 500 sheets measuring 24 x 36. It is expressly provided in the standard contract that the weight is to be determined without reference to the production basis, and that the paper is to be run as near to the weight as practicable, but 5 per cent, i. e., 1.6 pounds on 32, over or under the nominal weight shall be considered good delivery.

SPECIFICATION OF WIDTH.

There are over forty variations in the width of rolls, though usually they run from 74 inches full width to 62 or 63 inches, and then in fractions of an inch. The Standard contract proposes, as a uniform width, 66 inches, 49½ inches, 33 inches, subject to change only with the consent of the manufacturer.

PRICE.

Generally quoted on 100-pound basis.

Terms of payment.—Diversity has existed in the terms of payment: net cash in specified days from date of invoice; not later than specified date of succeeding month; 30 days from arrival of cars at destination, etc., are common. The standard form proposes net cash 30 days, or not later than the 15th of the month following shipment.

Freight.—Further standardization is made by fixing the price upon a mill basis, that is, f. o. b. at mill. The publisher thus stands the freight charges or is given an allowance therefor in the price. Under this arrangement, it follows that the purchaser makes his claims for damaged paper against the carrier, unless the paper was defective when it left the mill.

STORAGE.

The standard contract does not contain a "storage clause." The result is that the purchaser must provide his own storage.

STANDARD CONTRACT.

A new standard form of contract to cover deliveries in 1917 has been adopted by most of the news-print manufacturers. There are a few minor variations in the forms used by some of the manufacturers, but the principal provisions are substantially the same. A copy of the standard contract as proposed by the News Print Manufacturers Association is as follows:

STANDARD FORM OF CONTRACT.

IN CONSIDERATION of the mutual covenants and agreements hereinafter set out, THE STANDARD PAPER COMPANY, of the City of New York, State of New York, hereinafter called the SELLER, agrees to sell and hereby does sell, and THE NEWS PUBLISHING COMPANY of the City of New York, State of New York, hereinafter called the PURCHASER, agrees to buy and pay for, and hereby does buy, six hundred (600) tons of roll news print paper required to print editions of "The Morning News," a newspaper published in the City of New York, New York, during the period beginning January 1, 1916, and ending December 31, 1916, both dates inclusive, to be ordered and delivered in equal monthly installments of fifty (50) tons, not cumulative, subject to the following terms and conditions:

1. This contract, together with the TRADE CUSTOMS attached hereto and made a part hereof, is complete in itself, and sets forth the agreement, and conditions between the parties hereto, and it may not be assigned by either party except by consent of the other.

2. *Specification.*—A. The said paper shall be of substantially the same average quality as sample attached to this agreement and of approximately the following basis of weight: 24 x 36, 32/500, without reference to production basis.

B. Widths of rolls 66 inches, 49½ inches, 33 inches.

3. *Price.*—$2.68 per one hundred pounds actual weight of rolls, including paper and wrappers, but excluding cores, ON CARS AT MILL. Price includes freight allowance of 18 cents per one hundred pounds. Routing is reserved to the SELLER.[1]

4. *Terms.*—Net cash thirty (30) days from date of invoice, or not later than the 15th day of the month for all paper shipped the previous month. Payments shall be made in ——— Exchange.

5. *Delivery.*—The paper to be furnished under this agreement shall be the product of ——— with mills located at ———.

6. *Contingencies.*—In case the SELLER shall be unable and fail at any time to make and supply, or the PURCHASER shall be unable and fail to take and use said paper in consequence of strikes, fire, explosion, lock-outs, combinations of workmen, flood, drought, embargoes, war, the acts of God, the public enemy or any cause beyond the control of either party hereto, the SELLER shall not be liable to the PURCHASER for failure to supply such paper, nor shall the PURCHASER be liable to the SELLER for failure to take such paper during the period of the disability.

7. *Cancellation.*—If the PURCHASER shall fail to pay any amounts when due under this contract, or fail to make settlements as provided herein, the SELLER may, after ten (10) days written notice, cancel this contract and declare the obligations of the PURCHASER for all paper furnished hereunder due forthwith, notwithstanding the terms hereof, but the PURCHASER shall remain liable to the SELLER for all loss and damage sustained by reason of such failure.

---

[1] The new contract forms of one company contain the following provisions in regard to prices:

5. * * * (b) The above price of ——— net per one hundred pounds F. O. B. Mill to be adjusted annually proportionately up and down as the average aggregate cost to the mill of coal, wood and labor for each one hundred pounds of paper manufactured by the said mill varies each year, during the life of the contract, from the average aggregate cost to the mill of coal, wood and labor for each one hundred pounds manufactured by the mill for the first ten months of the calendar year 1916, the schedule of these costs for 1916 being attached hereto and both parties hereto certifying to the correctness thereof. The basis price of ——— net mill being made on the basis of costs for the first ten months of the calendar year 1916, this will be the cost schedule on which adjustments will be made each year. This clause of variation will also apply to any groundwood or sulphite pulp that the mill may have to buy outside, as compared to the mill's cost schedule through the mill's inability to manufacture in its own plant. Adjustment to be made by payment in cash by either side to the other on February 15, 1918, for the preceding year of 1917, and a like adjustment to be made on each succeeding February 15th for the preceding year following during the life of this contract.

6. * * * (b) In consideration of the fact that the price for paper above fixed is very greatly less than the price the Seller can obtain therefor if it limited the life of its contracts to a short period, and that the Seller is willing to and has sold said paper for said low price on condition that the Purchaser shall continue to purchase paper at the above price for the full term of this contract, the Purchaser agrees in case of its failure to take and pay for any of the paper purchased hereunder, or in case the Purchaser cancels this contract, to pay the liquidated damages hereinafter set forth for its breach or cancellation. Said liquidated damages shall be a sum equal to the difference between the price of the paper theretofore delivered hereunder computed on the basis of the present price which the seller is receiving for the same quality of paper from customers (which price is stipulated to be ——— per one hundred pounds F. O. B. Mill) and the price of the paper theretofore delivered hereunder computed on the basis of the contract price hereinbefore fixed. In the event of the breach or cancellation of this contract by the Purchaser, the obligation of the Purchaser shall be limited to pay the contract price hereinbefore fixed for paper theretofore delivered and the liquidated damages, hereinbefore set forth, the same to be the Seller's damages by reason of the Purchaser's refusal to continue to take the paper through the term and life of this contract.

THIS AGREEMENT is executed in duplicate original and shall be governed by the laws of the place of the legal domicile of the SELLER.

Executed at 100 Broadway, City, County and State of New York, this 10th day of December, 1915.

STANDARD PAPER COMPANY, SELLER,
By JOHN JOHNSON, *President.*

THE NEWS PUBLISHING COMPANY, PURCHASER,
By JOHN JONES, *President.*

ROLL NEWS PRINT PAPER TRADE CUSTOMS.

1. *Tonnage.*—PURCHASER shall order a definite tonnage of paper to be taken over the contract period and in equal monthly installments of the total contract tonnage.

2. *Basis of weight.*—Five per cent. (5%) over or under the contract basis of weight shall be considered good delivery.

3. *Widths.*—The widths of rolls mentioned in a contract are permanent unless the SELLER agrees to change.

4. *Specifications for shipments.*—The PURCHASER shall furnish to the SELLER by the 15th day of each month complete specifications for the shipments to be made the succeeding month.

5. *Weight.*—The weight of roll news print paper shall be gross weight less only the weight of cores.

6. *Delivery point.*—Delivery point is on board cars at place of manufacture.

7. *Terms.*—Terms net cash thirty days from date of invoice or not later than the 15th day of the month for all paper shipped the previous month.

8. *Cores.*—Cores shall be charged to the PURCHASER at one cent per inch if paper and three cents per inch if iron, and shall be returned promptly, freight prepaid, when they shall be credited to the PURCHASER at invoice price.

9. *Claims.*—A. No allowance shall be made for waste, damage or paper left on cores.

B. In case of claim of any nature applying upon any shipment of paper made under a contract, the SELLER shall be notified immediately, but no claim shall be allowed for consequential damage.

EXHIBIT 6.

CIRCULARS SENT OUT BY JOBBERS IN REGARD TO THE HIGH PRICES AND SCARCITY OF PAPER.

One of the questions in the schedule sent out by the Commission to newspaper publishers was as follows:

State reasons given you by seller for any recent increase in price of news print. Give full particulars, copies of correspondence, etc.

In response, many of the publishers sent in circular letters that they had received from jobbers. A number of these letters are given below.

[No. 1.]

SMITH, DIXON COMPANY,
DIVISION OF THE WHITAKER PAPER CO.,
Baltimore, January 17, 1916.

GENTLEMEN: While all prices are "subject to change without notice," this phrase is taking on a very definite meaning in these days, owing to conditions which the paper manufacturers of this country are facing.

Certain chemicals used in making paper, have been bought in enormous quantities by the manufacturers of high explosives; importations of other raw materials have stopped. The cost of these chemicals have advanced to a point never before reached, and in the case of some of them, there is no available supply at any price.

The paper mills are unable to contract at a fixed price for these products, and are forced to purchase as their needs demand at ever increasing prices. This accounts for the unstable paper market.

Unless otherwise instructed, we will charge all of your orders at our lowest current price, even if higher than you have paid on previous shipments. If we are forced to write you regarding every order received, waiting for your authority to charge at a higher price, the chances are that the price will be still higher by the time your answer reaches us.

Rest assured that no advantage will be taken of the conditions we are facing, and that no prices will be raised except where absolutely necessary.

Yours, very truly,

SMITH, DIXON COMPANY DIV.

[No. 2.]

WHY YOUR PAPERS COST YOU MORE.

Many buyers of paper are wondering if conditions justify the rapid advances that have been made, and will be made as long as the market remains in the present unsettled state.

The answer to these questions are the facts: that the paper manufacturers are compelled to advance prices, because of the high costs of raw materials, particularly of chemicals and dyes.

The table below shows the normal scale of prices, as compared to the prices that paper manufacturers are now paying for these same materials:

Bleached Sulphite	was $2.65 cwt.	Now	$3.75 to $4.25 cwt
Bleaching Powder	" 1¼ c.	"	13c. (and unobtainable)
Soda Ash	" 65 c. cwt.	"	2½c. "
Rosin	" 3.75 bbl.	"	6.50 bbl.
Satin White	" 5c. lb.	"	9c. lb.
Casein	" 6¼c. lb.	"	20 to 30 c. lb.
Alum	" 1c "	"	3c. "
Aniline Colors	" 40c. "	"	$20. "
Fourdrinier Wires	" 29c. sq. ft.	"	39c. sq. ft.
Woolen and Cotton Felts	have advanced 10%		
Thirds and Blues	was $1.35	"	2½ c.
Lumber (cases and frames)	" $13.25 M.	"	$18.50 M

Furthermore, the chemical people will not make any contracts at any price, so that mills are simply buying from hand to mouth, as their needs require, in many instances being unable to obtain certain supplies at any price.

As soon as conditions are normal, that is, when imports can be again resumed, or a larger domestic supply developed, prices will right themselves.

The chemicals used by paper manufacturers in making bleaching powder, have been bought in great quantities during the past few months by the makers of high explosives, so that this market has been very demoralized. This accounts for the shortage of supply, and the very high prices of such chemicals.

The higher prices now prevailing do not mean exorbitant profits to either the manufacturer or the paper dealer. It is a difficult thing to maintain even usual profits above the constantly rising costs.

SMITH, DIXON COMPANY DIV.,
Baltimore, Md.

FEBRUARY, 1916.

[No. 3.]

WEST-CULLUM PAPER COMPANY,
WHOLESALE PAPER FOR PRINTERS,
Dallas, Tex., February 24, 1916.

TO THE TRADE:

You have, no doubt, been keeping in pretty close touch with the condition of the paper industry, but thinking that many of our customers do not fully appreciate the seriousness of the situation, we have printed copies of a few letters such as we are receiving daily, as we believe the information will be worth something to the trade. You can readily see that it is impossible for any dealer to issue a price list which would be good even for a day, and that it will be necessary for us to bill orders at prices prevailing from day to day. We have access to the largest stocks of paper in the United States and it is not necessary for us to wait on mill orders to replenish our stock, which in many instances, would require three to four months' time. We believe we are in the best possible position to take care of the Texas trade, especially on small orders which are for immediate use, and feel that if you will entrust us with your orders, you will get quick service and the benefit of the best price to be had.

Very respectfully,

WEST-CULLUM PAPER COMPANY.

PLEASE NOTE: We think it will be worth your time to read carefully the enclosed copies, and to give same as much publicity as possible, in order to prepare your customers for the advance in prices, which you will be compelled to make.

—

SAINT LOUIS, *February 16, 1916.*

WEST-CULLUM PAPER Co., *Dallas, Texas.*

GENTLEMEN: In order to keep you posted on the paper situation, and in order that you may be thoroughly alive to the seriousness of the present market conditions we give you this letter. Conditions are growing worse daily. Many mills are facing the necessity of shutting down on account of lack of materials and the cost of every product which is used in the manufacture of paper has increased in price from 25% to 2000%.

In order that our customers may know the reasons for the existing conditions, and so they will appreciate the gravity of the situation, we give them the facts and figures. Here are the causes for the advancing prices:

FIRST. Increased cost of all materials used in making paper.

Rags	100% increase
Bleached Sulphite	formerly $45 ton, now $110
Soda Pulp	30% to 50% increase
Alum	300% to 400% increase
Rosin	40% increase
Wire Screen	25% to 50% increase
Felts	50% increase
Bleaching Powder	1000% increase and none to be had
Colors	500% to 2500% increase and up
Satin White	25% to 50% increase
Blanc Fix	100% to 150% increase
Casein	250% increase
Soda Ash	300% increase

Rags have advanced in price, both on account of short supply and the demand. Munition makers are using tremendous quantities of cotton rags to make explosives. Formerly we imported vast quantities of rags from Europe. This is all shut off. Russia uses linen almost as universally as we do cotton and a large proportion of our supply comes from there. None has been coming in for months and stocks are exhausted.

Chlorine (bleach) has advanced from 1¼c. a lb. to about 15c. a lb. on account of the stopping of supply from Europe and the domestic makers are busy with chlorine gas and chloroform.

SECOND. Decreased supply. You know the situation on colors.

Other paper ingredients are similarly affected by demand and supply. Before the war, Germany supplied a large part of the paper for the world, except to the United States, and even this country bought considerable paper and lots of pulp. Sweden also sold us large amounts of pulp, newspaper and wrapping—both countries making paper and pulp from Russian Wood.

Germany, of course, was shut out at once, but general business was so paralyzed all over the world that existing stocks of paper lasted for months and the loss of the German supply was not felt, while Sweden could continue to supply her share. After about one year, however, Swedish mills began to run out of wood, as on account of the conditions, they could not secure the usual amount from Russia so that cut off the Swedish supply.

Then European mills, formerly dependent on Germany and Sweden for pulp, turned to Canada, taking all the surplus Canadian pulp which formerly came to the United States. This caused a further shortage. To this trouble was added the high prices and scarcity of all chemicals and dyes, of which Germany formerly supplied us with the greater part. All these conditions making it increasingly difficult for the paper makers to secure supplies.

THIRD. Increased demand.

Just at the time that paper became scarce, there came a tremendous increase in business both here and in England and South America, creating an enormous and unheard of demand for paper. Stocks everywhere were short and there came a tremendous demand. Right on top of the shortage, South America, Asia, Australia and even some of the European countries began to buy paper in America, and to offer big premiums over existing prices.

The combined demand is for several times as much paper as American mills can make and the available supply of raw stock is very short and high in price, so it is no wonder prices are jumping.

There is no precedent for this present situation. We don't know where prices will go, but would not be surprised to see prices advance as much as 100%.

If your customers think the advances in paper are not reasonable, call their attention to the much greater increase in the price of all metals, electrical goods, all chemicals, woolen goods, and many others which have advanced very much more than paper.

Be exceedingly careful and warn all your salesmen not to take any orders for paper unless you are sure they can be shipped.

——

FEBRUARY 16, 1916.

WEST-CULLUM PAPER CO.,
    Dallas, Texas.

GENTLEMEN: To show my appreciation of the business you have given me in the past, I feel it is my duty to advise you of the seriousness of the situation with reference to paper; and give you such information as I can as to what you may expect in regard to price, and some of the reasons for the unprecedented advances which are already in effect and still greater advances which we may expect in the near future.

The paper trade is now facing an absolute famine and many mills will be forced to shut down on account of being unable to obtain rags, pulp, and chemicals. The largest mills in the country are refusing to make prices except at such prices as they may name upon receipt of the order at their mills, same being subject to their ability to make the paper at all. They will take no contracts nor orders for future delivery. The situation is desperate.

We have one letter from a big mill, stating they view the situation with the greatest alarm and believe we are going to see the most vicious market ever known. The largest aggregation of mills in the United States writes us as follows:

"Now in regard to entering future orders at the present prices, we cannot guarantee them at all, and prices are subject to acceptance at the prevailing prices on the day that the orders are received here. We know this is a terrible state of affairs and leaves you in a very unsatisfactory position, but you are not nearly as bad off as we are, because even where we have contracts for stock and material we cannot get them, and whenever we ask for any material, prices are quoted us subject to prior sale and advance without notice, and in many instances where we have received quotations and wired acceptance of them we have been notified the stock had all been sold, so you can see we cannot guarantee our prices, even from one day to another."

Now, the fact is, there is a tremendous demand for paper, a shortage of materials with high prices and a wild scramble to secure such materials as are yet to be obtained. Many dealers will be out of paper unless something unforeseen occurs and every indication is that prices will continue to advance rapidly and that paper will get scarcer until an actual famine exists and that many buyers will be unable to secure their necessary supply.

We will put forth every effort to secure enough paper to keep our old customers supplied. We don't want to sell any one buying large amounts, but expect to split up our stock among our regular customers to keep them supplied as far as possible. Therefore, we are not making any lower prices for large quantities than we could for case lots. Our object is to take care of our regular trade and not try to take advantage of the situation to get new customers, because the mills are now in a panic because they cannot get material to fill orders and are lying down on their contracts. We think we are in better position to take care of our customers than the majority of our competitors on account of the large stocks we always carry and believe we will be in a better position to fill orders than many of our competitors for the reason that we have tied up with mills that are best fixed to run during this famine. By our policy we hope to have a lot of loyal friends among our customers for the reason that we have taken care of them when no one else could. We are not soliciting large orders for future use.

We believe you are going to see some fire works in the paper market soon. Our positive instructions are not to tie up on any big business and none of our salesmen have authority to bind our house on any agreement as all orders are taken subject to acceptance by the house. So it will be necessary for us to consult the St. Louis Office before accepting any large orders, and we cannot take any future orders without authority from St. Louis— not even carloads. Any of our customers who will place their orders with us and allow us to place them at the best prices obtainable, will, I think, in the long run, fare better and be better taken care of than the ones not fortunate enough to be on our books as our good friends.

In another letter I give you some of the causes of these advances as your salesmen may not be fully posted and you can give this letter to them so they can answer inquiries from their customers. We wish this letter to be notice to you that, while we will be glad to take care of your orders and believe we will be able to take care of them fairly well, that all former prices are absolutely withdrawn, and we can only quote you from day to day. A better plan would be for you to place your orders with us and we will agree to handle them for you on a reasonable profit and place them at the lowest possible market price the day we receive the order.

———

[No. 4.]

THE CLEMENTS PAPER COMPANY,
WHOLESALE PAPER,
Nashville, Tenn.

TO OUR CUSTOMERS:

On account of the extraordinary conditions now existing in the paper industry, all orders are accepted subject to prices prevailing at time of shipment, to change without notice and to our ability to secure stock.

Mills are filled with orders and are refusing to take any new business, and it is not as much a question of price as it is to get stock within a reasonable time, and we are not certain just what the cost will be on many items.

There is a shortage of wood pulp, rags and chemicals used in paper making, and paper mill workers have been given shorter hours and higher wages. Unfortunately this country has been dependent on foreign countries for a large part of their raw material, and prices have advanced to the highest level ever known.

Prices in general have advanced approximately 30% on most of the staple items used by printers, and we will issue a circular as soon as practicable giving more in detail the changes that are taking place.

Under existing conditions we are trying to give the best service and as accurate information in regard to the market as can be obtained. Your customers will be fortunate for the next few months in getting the kind of paper they desire, even at the advanced prices you will be forced to charge them.

Yours, truly,

CLEMENTS PAPER COMPANY.

MARCH 24, 1916.

[No. 5.]

TEMPORARY NET PRICE LIST, ISSUED APRIL 15, 1916.

NOTE.—Use our Fall 1915 List for Sizes, Weights and Descriptions, but THIS LIST for Guidance on Prices.

It is generally known how seriously the cost end of the paper manufacturing business has been directly and indirectly affected by affairs in Europe.

Materials used in paper making, such as dye stuffs, bleaching powder and sulphite pulp, soda ash, rags, casein and the numerous other ingredients have had many sharp price advances. In addition to this, the demand is far in excess of normal. Hence it is obvious that under prevailing conditions there can be no stability in the selling prices of paper.

This Temporary Price List represents the latest word in prices at the time of going to press, but we are obliged to notify you that due to uncertainty, all prices are subject to change without notice. You are assured, however, that we will always give you the very best quotations on all orders entrusted to us.

PRICES SUBJECT TO CHANGE WITHOUT NOTICE.

J. W. BUTLER PAPER COMPANY,
(Established 1844.)   *Chicago.*

———

[No. 6.]

OKLAHOMA CITY, OKLA,. *June 24, 1916.*

GENERAL LETTER NO. 58.

GENTLEMEN: The News Print Situation is getting worse instead of better and several of the mills are going out of the Print business— Kimberly-Clark Co., Rhinelander and Dells Pulp & Paper Co., three of the largest print mills are discontinuing the print business and nearly all the other mills are snowed under.

Therefore, owing to the stiff advance put on paper and scarcity at the present time, we have found it necessary to advance our prices as follows, effective June 26, 1916:

Ton lots	5 00
1,000 lbs.	5 10
500 "	5 25
Bdl lots	5 40
Ream lots	5 85
Brkn "	6 85

These prices are all f. o. b. Okla. City.

If we can not get this price for print paper we want to pass up the business. Our supply is getting very limited and we have promised only one car for July, and may possibly get a car in August, which is the only stock we have in sight. We want to take care of our regular customers as far as possible, so do not take on any new print business, if you can avoid it.

In a letter I received from I. W. Carpenter he stated he had just bought two cars on the 14th, for which he was obliged to pay $3.95.

Yours, very truly,

KANSAS CITY PAPER HOUSE,
L. F. LEACH, Jr.

———

[No. 7.]

OMAHA, NEB., *June 27, 1916.*

GENTLEMEN: I returned home Thursday morning from about a week's trip thruout the paper making district of Minnesota and Wisconsin. I thought you might be interested in a general way in some things which I learned on this trip.

There was a slight rumor about a possibility of an advance on flat writing papers and bond papers, but I have advised some manufacturers I have seen strongly against it and I hope it will not come at this time.

I find the market on book paper especially stiff. The price went up half a cent per pound at three different mills on Wednesday of last week and I find the book paper mills crowded with business, most of them having sixty days' business on their books and not desiring orders at the present prices.

I find the news print situation quite serious on account of three large mills making an aggregate of one hundred tons per day are arranging to discontinue making news print and get on more profitable lines. This taken together with the increased consumption of news print by the Metropolitan dailies causes a shortage in the supply to provide for the demand. Hence, the present tremendous prices the mills are asking and getting for paper.

In our experience in business in Omaha of nearly thirty years we have never encountered anything like the present conditions. In our judgment it would be well for all users of news print to cut down as much as possible their consumption for a few months or until the war is over. A good suggestion from the manufacturer was that the publisher pass this advance on to the advertiser in slightly increased rates on advertising. It is absolutely necessary that all printers pass on the increased cost of paper on job work. Is it not worth while to increase also your prices on advertising enough to cover the increased cost of news print?

Another thing which has contributed to the high price of paper is the foreign demand. I am told that during the first four months of 1915 we exported 5,000,000 pounds of printing paper and during the same period in 1916 we exported 35,000,000 pounds of printing paper, and we had offered to us more than ten times as much as was accepted by the American mills. The European war has brought about the above change in international commerce.

In our judgment then nothing short of peace in Europe will restore prices on all grades of printing paper to anything like normal conditions.

Hoping your customers will receive the necessary advances graciously, and with kind regards, we are,

Yours truly,

CARPENTER PAPER CO.

[No. 3.]

TO THE TRADE:

JULY 21, 1916.

Mill prices have again been withdrawn and as a consequence we are compelled to cancel all outstanding quotations and prices listed in our General Catalog No. 10 and our Supplementary Price List No. 27. Until a new schedule of prices can be arranged we will quote only on application.

Your indulgence during these unsettled times is requested.

Yours, truly,

ZELLERBACH PAPER COMPANY,
Los Angeles : San Diego.

JULY 21, 1916.

Owing to the continued advances in the price of papers of all grades and the increasing scarcity of raw materials, we find it necessary to withdraw all prices.

A new price list is now being printed, and until this reaches you we will be glad to quote on request.

BLAKE, MOFFITT & TOWNE,
Los Angeles.

Effective Saturday, July 22, 1916.

The continued disturbed condition among paper manufacturers becomes more aggravated daily, thereby creating a shortage in practically all kinds of paper to an extent that compels the mills to make further substantial advances, and, under these circumstances, we are obliged to withdraw all outstanding quotations and prices, and until a new list can be issued we assure you that on all orders intrusted to us the lowest market prices will be charged.

SIERRA PAPER COMPANY,
126–130 S. Los Angeles St., Los Angeles, Cal.

[No. 9.]

BUY NOW.

The print paper market shows no improvement and stocks are depleted generally. We will have another car tomorrow and can accept your order for immediate shipment, subject to prior sale, on the following sizes and weights at 5½c. Des Moines, for standard grade:

24 ×35–32   35×48–64
30½×44–50   35×44–58

The situation is more critical today than ever and it is good business to buy now while you can get it at any price.

WESTERN NEWSPAPER UNION,
Des Moines, Iowa.

JULY 28, 1916.

[No. 10.]

D. L. WARD COMPANY,
MANUFACTURERS AND DISTRIBUTERS,
OFFICES, 28 SOUTH SIXTH STREET,
WAREHOUSES, 238–240 QUEEN STREET,
Philadelphia, Pa.

GENTLEMEN: *Paper conditions.*—In answer to such questions as "What are the causes for the present high prices of paper?" "When do you think prices will decline?" which I am being constantly asked as a distributer of paper, and as often asking myself, as a buyer of the same commodity, I submit a few facts that stand out as the important causes for the present situation.

First. A large proportion of bleached and unbleached sulphite and ground-wood pulp that we use in the manufacture of paper, has come from Europe. The amount from Central Empires has been entirely stopped, while the pulp from Norway and Sweden has materially decreased. What we are receiving is costing double its former value, due to the present cost of coal, labor, ocean freight rate, and steamship insurance.

Rags.—Fifty per cent of our supply of rags comes from Europe.

Chemicals.—Dyes, chemicals, felts, paper machinery and in fact every other article which goes into the manufacture of paper, has increased anywhere from twice to ten times the price paid one year ago.

Labor.—Labor has increased twenty-five to fifty per cent, due to the fact that practically all mills have replaced the two-tour system with the three, requiring three sets of workmen instead of two. In many localities the present scale of wages that munition factories have set, has had to be competed with.

Demand.—The demand for paper has increased thirty per cent. In my opinion, one half of this increase is actual consumption, which will continue as long as we have the present prosperity. The other is speculative buying by all types of paper consumers. This, due to the present high prices, will naturally discontinue. This will result to the advantage of both seller and buyer.

High prices.—The above answers the first question, to the best of my ability, as to what causes the present high prices of paper.

Second.—As to when prices will decline, if you believe the above information, I am sure you will agree, only after the end of the present European war. It will then take some time for prices to adjust themselves because Europe's pulp supply is greatly dependent on the supply of logs from Russia, and no trees have been cut in the last year. It will therefore be six months to a year before there will be any steady relief in sight. It is quite unlikely that the paper mills will ever be able to go back to the two-tour or twelve-hour day in regard to labor. It is for this reason that I doubt that we shall ever see the former abnormally low prices.

Experience.—An experience as a very large buyer and seller of practically all types of paper, and an intimate associate with nearly all large manufacturers, leads me to answer both questions quoted as above for the guidance of my customers and others interested in the purchase of paper.

Yours very truly,

D. L. WARD COMPANY,
GEORGE W. WARD, *President.*

AUGUST TENTH, 1916.

P. S.—By way of comparison, I submit the following table of importation of sulphite:

Importation of sulphite for year.

	Tons.
1912	354,000
1913	373,466
1914	458,156
1915	394,321

Contrast this table with the imports to date this year:

Imports of sulphite by months for 1916, from Europe.

	Tons.
January	28,830
February	31,972
March	15,091
April	9,270
May	3,982

O